PURPLE PROSE

PURPLE PROSE

Liz Byrski and Rachel Robertson

 FREMANTLE PRESS

Contents

Introduction – Liz Byrski and Rachel Robertson 7

The Things I Cannot Say – Natasha Lester 11
Maiden Aunts – Liz Byrski 22
Blue Meat and Purple Language – Toni Jordan 36
Into the Whipstick – Anne Manne 45
Velvet – Rachel Robertson 60
'Is a Magnificent Story': Interviews with Pigeon Fanciers –
   Sarah Drummond 72
Do You See What I See? – Tracy Farr 83
Mary – Lucy Dougan 95
The Trouble with Purple – Annamaria Weldon 105
The Red and the Blue: Confessions of an (Unlikely)
   Dockers Fan – Deborah Hunn 116
The Two Loves – Lily Chan 132
Purple Impressions – Rosemary Stevens 139
Bruised – Jacqueline Wright 148
My Descent into Purple – Hanifa Deen 162
Towards Metamorphosis – Amanda Curtin 175

Notes and References....................................187
Contributors 196

Introduction – Liz Byrski and Rachel Robertson

'Writing, when properly managed (as you may be sure I think mine is) is but a different name for conversation ...'
Laurence Sterne, *The Life and Opinions of Tristram Shandy*

Purple Prose began with a conversation between two friends over a cup of tea in Liz's herb-scented courtyard. One of us – Rachel – wanted to write about purple, but she couldn't think how to do it. She didn't think she could write a whole book about the colour. Then Liz suggested an anthology of women writing about purple, and we agreed that this could work and was something we wanted to do. We both have our own histories and associations with purple, but an important one was purple as a feminist colour and this was why we envisaged a book by women.

We went away to do some research on purple and found that it was just as interesting as we suspected. Culturally, purple is associated with many different things across different cultures, including penitence, mourning, harmony, royalty, feminism, women's suffrage, lesbian, gay and transgender rights, wealth, healing, and spirituality.

There are a surprising number of purple flowers, vegetables, insects and animals. Creatures like the Indian purple frog, the purple heron, the purple queenfish and the purple sea urchin are all actually purple. There are purple minerals too: amethyst, porphyry, lavender chalcedony, lepidolite, purple jade, lavender jasper, purpurite, tanzanite. There is even a rare purple mineral first identified in Australia. Stichtite, a magnesium, chromium carbonate-hydroxide, was discovered in Australia in 1891 and named in 1910.

Tyrian purple is a dye extracted from a mollusc found on the shores of the ancient city of Tyre in Phoenicia around the time of the Minoan civilisation. The difficulty of extracting the dye and the number of molluscs required meant that only rich people could use the dye, thus creating a connection between wealth or royalty and purple. The Chinese developed a synthetic purple barium copper silicate pigment, known as Han purple, as early as 1045 BCE and used it to colour beads, pottery, ceramics and wall paintings until the end of the Han Dynasty. More recently, the synthetic organic chemical dye, mauveine, was discovered by accident by Dr William Henry Perkin in 1856 while he was trying to make quinine.

In scientific terms, purple, unlike violet, is not one of the colours of the visible spectrum. Because it does not have its own wavelength of light, it is called a non-spectral colour. In colour theory, purple is a colour existing between violet and red (excluding violet and red themselves). But nowadays, violet, indigo, lilac and all other shades between red and blue are generally called purple. In discussing our anthology inspired by purple, we decided not to be constrained by specific varieties of or associations to the colour, but to give ourselves a free rein.

Once we had our theme, we had another conversation in another garden, this time over coffee with Georgia Richter, publisher and editor at Fremantle Press. We were delighted that Georgia was enthusiastic about our project. We approached some of our favourite women writers and asked them to contribute a piece of memoir or a personal essay inspired by purple. The writers we contacted were all people whose work we knew and admired and who we guessed would in some way respond to the idea of writing about the colour. The writers are diverse in age, background and life paths but still, we worried that we might receive lots of pieces about purple as a feminist and suffragette colour or about the book *The Color Purple* by Alice Walker.

INTRODUCTION

Our worries were unnecessary. What was astounding to us was the diversity of responses to a single writing prompt. The way each woman approached the task and the way her personal life and purple intersect is remarkably different, and equally fascinating. But there are some themes that emerge from the collection. First there is the theme of transformation – how we change and how we struggle to change. We start the collection with a work that demonstrates the interwoven complexities of gender and identity, of change and continuity. We end the book with a very different exploration of transformation, the metamorphosis that occurs with experience and reflection.

Travel, through time and space, features in many of these works. Family stories, memory and forgetting emerge as women explore their roles as mothers, sisters, daughters and grand-daughters. Wisps of purple fabric rustle through the book in the probing of women's relationships with other family members. Several contributors reflect purple's connection to spirituality and others its strong link with loss. There are stories about childhood, about gender, and about ageing. Passions like football, art and pigeon-racing are also explored in this book. Contributors investigate the way we see the world and the way we write about this.

A year on from our initial conversation, we sat again with cups of tea, this time by Rachel's fish pond, and we read the fifteen contributions that make up this book. Apart from the colour purple, we recognised that each of these works is about how we make our lives into stories and how that makes our lives richer. Our conversation with each other has become a wider conversation with all our writers and, we hope, our readers.

Our final conversation is about the title. We originally used the working title of *Purple Prose* as a sort of joke, referring to over-elaborate or ornate writing. But one of the contributors alerts us to the fact that the phrase 'purple language' has been used to refer also to highly colourful swearing. We like the transgressive (and Shandyesque playfulness) of calling women's writing purple in this way, so we decide to stick with *Purple Prose*. We hope readers will embrace the energy, the colour, and the stories to be found in this book.

The Things I Cannot Say – Natasha Lester

'Bless you, my darling, and remember you are always in the heart – oh tucked so close there is no chance of escape – of your sister.'
     Katherine Mansfield, *Collected Letters*

My favourite book as a girl was Louisa May Alcott's *Little Women*. I loved Amy March. In fact, I wanted to be Amy with her curly blonde hair, blue eyes, artistic temperament, delusions of grandeur and a house full of sisters.

On the cover of my thirty-five-year-old copy of *Little Women*, Amy is wearing a purple dress picked out with white polka dots, and a purple bonnet trimmed with white lace. Her sister Beth is also in purple, although her dress is more demure and covered with a housewifely apron. Purple in all its shades follows the sisters throughout the book; the slippers Beth embroiders for Mr Laurence are deep purple, Amy bequeaths Mr Laurence her purple box with looking glass when she writes out her will, Meg yearns for a violet silk dress, and Jo's shabby poplin dress that she wears to the ball is deep maroon. It's no wonder that when I think of purple, I think of *Little Women*. And when I think of *Little Women*, I think of sisters.

*

On weekends, from the time I was around six to the time I was eleven, my sister and I used to play with our dolls. We concocted elaborate games for our ratty collection of plastic children to participate in. One of our favourite games was hospitals. My sister and I were the doctors, the dolls were the patients.

In an old indigo-covered school exercise book we wrote lengthy descriptions of invented diseases, accompanied by illustrations showing the manifestation of each disease in all its putrid glory. We gave the illnesses names like the deadly Gangalknee Virus and the frightening Amoebic Pustitis, which made one's throat swell to a point that the patient suffocated and died in a breathless purple fit. Each day of the weekend, my sister and I would walk down the rows of beds in our makeshift hospital. We examined each doll with our plastic tweezers, applied fraying bandages, consulted our diagnostic manual, treated those who could be saved and sighed over those who couldn't.

Our dolls would all recover or be resurrected by four o' clock Sunday because that was when pack-up time commenced. Even now, 4.00 pm on a Sunday still carries with it a sense of loss, of playtime prematurely shut down, of an exchange of the possibilities of imagination for the realities of homework, dinner and hair-washing. I always thought my sister felt the same as I about both the games and their cessation until she brutally announced, a couple of weeks after she started high school, that she didn't want to play with dolls any more. I was shocked. It had never occurred to me that doll-playing wasn't a lifetime's work. That the carefully drawn diagrams of disease would be left in a desk to yellow and fade, that the dolls would sit gathering dust in their hair until they were tossed away, too well-loved to be given to the poor.

It was the first time I felt bewildered by my sister's behaviour. It was the first time I felt absence as palpable, defined not just by what wasn't there – the camaraderie of playing together in our childish hospital – but also by what was there: a new person, a sister I was unacquainted with. Prior to that, we'd been exactly as I imagined sisters to be. We played together like Beth and Amy in *Little Women* with their own worn-out dolls. We fought together like Jo and Amy, except our battles were less devilish, consisting only of slapping one another until we both began to cry, rather than burning manuscripts. We talked together about the complexities of the world – was God really everywhere, even in our mouths? – like Jo and Meg do after a night out dancing. We even had matching clothes and possessions, either because we both liked the same things or because it was easier for adults to assume that we did when they were buying for us.

For instance, my grandmother made us matching party dresses every year. I have a photograph of my sister and me wearing purple corduroy dresses, pink tights and maroon Mary-Jane shoes. We were both given a jewellery box for our birthdays that year, with a twirling ballerina on a circular stand. Mine played 'Für Elise'. My sister's played the theme from *Love Story*. How she must have hated the little-girlishness of it, the ballerina's tulle skirt, the romantic cliché of the music and the lavender velvet lining of the jewellery box, designed to hide and protect everything from secrets to sequins. They were all the things I loved.

*

My brother lives a couple of hours out of the city. I rarely see him. For us to meet, I would have to drive to his house, taking my three children with me. I would have to leave them in the car while I knocked at my brother's door for as long as it took him to cover his skin with trousers, socks, a long-sleeved shirt, mittens and a hat. It wouldn't matter if it were forty degrees outside. He would still cover up.

I would not be allowed into his house. We would have a conversation in the doorway, with me trying to find out how he was in between shouting at my three-year-old not to pull his sisters' hair. That is the best I could hope for. So I rarely invest the four-hour drive there and back for so little reward. He won't answer the phone. He used to write letters, so we could correspond, but not any more. Occasionally, he will answer an email.

He is on antidepressants and antipsychotics, has been in and out of the psychiatric ward of the hospital three or four times during the last year for anorexia and other problems, has not had a job for more than twelve years, has no friends, speaks to no one. He occupies his time planning and executing detailed combat manoeuvres against his bitter foes, Dirt and Germs, or cosseting his best friends, Imaginary Mortal Illnesses.

*

As I write this, it is as if I am inventing a character in a novel. My brother sounds like an oddity, a curiosity after whom people occasionally enquire with the same degree of interest that might be invoked by the discovery of a new breed of housefly. He is my children's uncle but they hardly know him. How do you explain, to a three, a five and a seven-year-old, that he thinks kids are a red-alert on the germ scale, second only to dogs?

But he isn't a curiosity, and despite the long drive, the indifferent reception I would receive, the complications my three children present, I know I should do more. Because my brother was, once upon a time, my sister. My best friend. The person I would have done anything for.

*

I watch my daughters play with their dolls. The handsome prince is being baked in the oven again because of some unspecified naughtiness. One of the girls is in charge of the roasting time, the other is preparing the dungeon, which is the poor prince's final resting place. They are taking turns to create the game, they giggle together at one another's ideas, they shriek at the fun of pretending to saw the prince's legs off with a plastic knife. My eldest daughter sneaks glances at me to see if I am about to step in and defend the prince and stop the game.

At one point, she hugs her sister and says, 'I love you, Audrey.'

As I watch, I wish for them a shared future of laughter, shrieking and camaraderie in sisterly adventures that involve such things as chopping up the limbs of feckless boyfriends. They will burn each other's manuscripts but quench their hatred when one of them disappears beneath cracked ice. They will tramp through miles of mud when one is sick and far from home. They will push each other off a ledge, not just to see what happens, but to make the other see too, just as sisters do in stories, and sometimes, perhaps, in real life.

But I don't really know what sisters do in real life. Because I no longer have a sister. In her place, I have a brother. My sister became my brother about fifteen years ago, a transition that was both a surprise and not a surprise all at the same time. Because something was clearly wrong. She was withdrawn, antisocial, rarely worked, silent. She was locked in a body she hated, jailed by a gender she had not chosen.

How astonishing then, for someone who so rarely spoke, to make such a bold declaration to the world. Bold because, at the time, and still now, it was such a uncommon thing to do, to change gender. It was a thing not talked about, a thing thought by many to be deviant or taboo. I know this because I've seen the way people avoid speaking about my sister and my brother, as if the person she was and the person he has become have both ceased to exist.

*

I have left several selves behind me, selves I can hardly remember being. They are like the events connected to photographs in my childhood album – I know they existed because I have the evidence of them but I cannot imagine that I was ever that person.

These selves seem unconnected physically from me, although they linger in my memory: the fifteen-year-old girl so enamoured with what her friends thought that she had no opinions of her own; the twenty-five-year-old woman singing her heart out at a Robbie Williams concert at Wembley Stadium; the twenty-eight-year-old bride who had not yet encountered her own children and could therefore not imagine loving anyone else the way she loved her husband.

But my shearing off is metaphorical. I have not had to surgically remove those selves. They have slipped away with the passage of time, without causing me bodily injury. My brother has had to hollow himself out, to cut off the physical manifestations of the person he can no longer bear to be. He has had to be counselled, operated on, had to fill out dozens of pieces of paperwork and explain to countless organisations that he can no longer tick the 'female' box when it comes to expressing himself to the world. Because the world lets us know, in countless tiny ways, that we must always have a declared gender and that gender, once granted, is part of our personhood.

A sister, for instance, is a female person, a 'daughter of the same parents', according to my *Macquarie Dictionary* in a typically unimaginative description. But what else is a sister? My intellectual self wants to run to the literature, to hide behind someone else's words and emotionless theories of sisterhood. Because then I would never have to say that when I found out my sister was going to live life as a man, my wedding was about a month away. My first thought was that people would encounter him in his men's clothes and with a dusky wash of stubble at my wedding for the first time and I would have to explain it. Why should I have to explain anything on a day that was supposed to be all about me?

As soon as I thought it, I pretended I hadn't and was horrified at my own selfishness. Because obviously my wedding was going to be the first of many occasions when my brother would find himself in a room full of people who would whisper about him but who would not ask him their questions directly. He was trapped in a new awkwardness, an awkwardness again not of his choosing. This time, the awkwardness was manifested by other people who wanted to study him but didn't know where to look, who wanted to brand him as confused or just plain weird, who wondered how anyone could do something so unimaginable, and who thanked God that their own siblings were 'normal'.

The awkwardness I felt was of a different kind. I wondered if I could acknowledge what had happened, talk about it with him, ask him questions. But I was a reminder of what he used to be. I was attached to the person he wanted to leave behind. Talking about it with him reminded him of the girl he wanted to forget, the girl he hated. The girl he wished had never existed.

How can I be so selfish as to want to remember a sister my brother loathed?

*

I feel guilty for mourning my sister. Guilty because mourning implies sadness. I worry that being sad suggests I do not support my brother's decision. I should focus on what I've gained, not what I've lost. I should see the rainbow and not the rain. So I never grieved for her, in case that grief was misconstrued as grief over my brother's decision, rather than over loss. A person still exists who is made of the same atoms as my sister. So what is there to lament? Then I read Rebecca Goldstein's attempts to unpick the complexities of personal identity and it was a revelation. She articulates exactly what I could not: 'A person whom one has loved seems altogether too significant a thing to simply vanish altogether from the world. A person whom one loves is a world, just as one knows oneself to be a world. How can worlds like these simply cease altogether?'

Indeed, how can they? But they do. I know my sister has vanished, has ceased. She will never come again.

In *Little Women*, Beth's death is a 'benignant angel – not a phantom full of dread'. Birds sing over her soul. In dying, 'Beth was well at last.' I hoped that becoming a man would heal my sister, that her metaphorical death would be that same benignant angel. That my new brother would be able to have conversations with people, would be able to work, would even find love. I hoped it would tweezer out the pain of the previous twenty-five years of being thought of as one thing, the wrong thing. That it might bandage up the deep wounds caused by thousands of thoughtless actions – the gifts of dresses and dolls and jewellery boxes from well-meaning relatives – and my own actions as a child in casting her as the ideal sister from a storybook, which was the exact opposite of who he wanted to be.

I wanted my brother to become someone who could smile occasionally, someone who would answer the telephone, someone who might venture outside into the sunshine. But that never happened. Instead he became more withdrawn, overcome with fears and phobias about dirt and illness, unable to eat, anorexic, declared mentally unable to work, alive only in the mechanical sense that his heart continues to beat and his brain stem allows him to perform the basic tasks of movement and breathing.

I've tried to do what I thought was right. I've put away the photos of my sister, I never speak about our childhood except in the vaguest possible terms, I tell everyone that I have two brothers and no sisters. On the rare occasions when I see him, I say hello and he nods at me. He doesn't speak, ever.

I wonder at what he cannot say.

*

'One is not born, but rather becomes a woman,' Simone de Beauvoir states in *The Second Sex* and the thinker in me understands the notion that gender is socially and culturally ascribed, whereas sex relates to the anatomical body one is born with. But gender is one of the primary labels we attach to people. We immediately identify people as woman or man based on the way they look. Ideas of gender are assumed to shift and change over time as society and culture changes, but, regardless, one's sex and one's gender are thought by most people to be fixed and the same. If someone looks like a man, they are assumed to be a man both physically and categorically.

To change one's gender – the M or F label they tick on a box on a form – and their sex – their physical body – requires medication, psychological assessments and staged surgery so that one's anatomy remains, for a time, in a state of flux. In fact it often remains forever in a liminal space because the final stage of gender reassignment surgery is far too costly for most people, including my brother, to consider. But, as well as this, it requires a change of name on all documents validating one's identity. It requires new clothing, new hairdos. It requires everybody who knew what you once were to remember to use the pronoun 'he' rather than the pronoun 'she' and, after nearly thirty years, this is a hard habit to break.

How many times have I heard relatives, my parents, myself in the first few months, accidentally say 'she'. How it must have hurt my brother each time we did. But that is just one of the small shifts required. The bigger shift is to realise how hard it is for someone to change gender and sex, but still have the world treat them the same as anybody else.

If one is not born a woman, but then becomes a woman, that is the way our gendered society largely expects one will stay. These expectations have been so damaging to my already fragile brother. I imagine he sees how easily other categories in our lives can be changed – I shifted from marketer to writer, from daughter to mother – and these changes were celebrated, and even expected as part of my growing up. I announced the new label I was to give myself – 'I'm going to be a mum!' – we raised our glasses, moved on and no further explanations were required, the evidence of my children being enough to testify to my new state of being. But, fifteen years ago, nobody popped a champagne bottle to salute my brother's more courageous and more significant transformation.

In fact, for some people, my brother's decision to inhabit one box instead of another still has the dark cloak of a secret about it. Recently, my mum gave me some of the books we used to have as children, for me to pass on to my children. She opened the front cover of one, pointed to a white streak of liquid paper on the title page and said, 'I whited out her name.' (It was a book that had been my sister's.) My mum continued, 'Because you wouldn't be able to explain to your kids who this person was.'

In one sense, my mother was right. But she meant it in a different way. She meant that explaining to my children that their uncle used to be a girl would be an impossible thing. Why? Kids are probably the best people to tell. They accept that almost anything is possible, even fairies.

My mother was right only in the sense that, for me, the fact I am still holding on to the sister I used to have is the one thing I cannot say.

*

I'm aware of how I must sound. As if I'm complaining, when it's my brother who has had so much more to bear. It's why I go along with the pretence that my whole childhood is an invention, a dream of weekend games, a story of lying beneath a purple quilt in a shared bedroom and having whispered conversations as we read the same Enid Blytons one after the other, about what boarding school might be like.

My games were played, my conversations were had with a ghost-girl who still haunts me. My sister is a secret I must keep close, hidden in my heart. It is the only place where I can stop pretending, where I can remember that once, long ago, my sister really did exist.

*

And then comes a breakthrough. My brother has moved back in with my parents for a short time. There is an issue to do with my parents' unwillingness to explain to some of their old friends the new state of things with my brother. Of course, it isn't a *new* state given it's been this way for fifteen years but my parents are still unable to talk about it.

I'm shocked. Driven by this, I reach out to my brother again and we begin an email correspondence. He asks what books my children would like for Christmas. I try to make sure he doesn't rush into a rental tenancy that isn't right for him. It is like thin ice, this correspondence. Shards of our renewed relationship might break off at any moment. But there is also beauty reflected there, in the possibility of the ice strengthening, of not breaking, of a new world of love forming.

Maiden Aunts – Liz Byrski

It's on a cold grey afternoon, a couple of weeks before Christmas 1949, that I first meet the maiden aunts. I'm five years old and grumpy after the long drive from Surrey to the East End of London through the Blackwall Tunnel; Dad behind the wheel, Mum alongside him and me whining in the back. Dad pulls up outside a two-storey terraced house in Hackney, and I see a woman's face looking out between the lace curtains.

'Aunt Lil's spotted us,' Dad says. He turns to me. 'Best behaviour now,' he says as the woman appears at the front door. 'Can you remember their names?'

I recite the names: Olive, Violet, Gladys and Lily. I've heard them often enough, always in this order, listed by my parents and their sister-in-law, my paternal grandmother. Until today I have only known one real aunt and one pretend one, and now I am getting a job lot of four. They are Dad's aunts really, my great-aunts, but in my very limited experience aunts mean presents and so grumpiness turns to anticipation.

Aunt Lil is short and thickset with fuzzy reddish hair flecked with grey. She is dressed entirely in black, with a white lace collar, and wears round spectacles with metal frames. When she bends to pat me on the cheek I notice that there is ink on the first two fingers of her right hand.

'Last time I saw you was at your christening,' she says. 'You were just a baby then.' And she leads us in through the front door along a passage lined with pressed tin and painted in an ugly tobacco brown, through to a large room with French doors leading out to a neat patch of garden. There are comfy chairs, an upright piano, and yes – a huge aspidistra in a brass pot. From its perch in a cylindrical cage a large black minah bird glares at us with beady eyes. The round table is set for tea with fine china, plates of tiny triangular sandwiches, and a three-tier cake stand loaded with scones and cakes.

Standing with her back to the fireplace is Aunt Gladys, wearing a dress in maroon crepe and a handsome string of pearls. She is a couple of years older than Lily and they are so much alike that they could be taken for twins. Beside her is Olive, the eldest of the four, shorter than her two younger sisters, and shaped like a cottage loaf, with iron grey hair twisted in to a tight bun on top of her head. She is wearing a dull brown dress covered in a floral wraparound overall. I am drawn to her immediately as she looks very much like Mrs Smith who comes to clean for Mum, and who, despite the fact that sweets are still on ration, always carries a supply of toffees in her overall pocket.

Memory is such a fickle beast; it scatters the past with its broken glass, a mix of sharp and dazzling shards and misty powdered fragments. Snatches of that afternoon are clear as yesterday, the rest just vague impressions: the trio of aunts, the piano, the ugly aspidistra and the scary minah with its raucous squawks. I can almost feel the tension – the awkwardness of relatives who rarely see each other and have little or nothing in common. I am hugged and kissed and Olive gives me a peppermint lump. I am soon bored; there is too much talking and not enough action. The minah glares at me and I glare back, but my thoughts are with the cakes, the box of chocolates on the piano, and those tantalising presents in the corner.

There are questions about Vi, the fourth aunt, and whether or not she will make an appearance. I have just completed my first term at a Catholic convent and am enchanted by the story of the Virgin Mary appearing to St Bernadette of Lourdes. Will Aunt Vi's appearance be similar – a vision out of nowhere, hands clasping a rosary? Will I too become a saint when I have seen her?

Eventually Olive gets up. 'I'll make the tea,' she says heading for the kitchen, but stops at the foot of the stairs.

'Vi,' she calls, 'Vi, they're here, I'm making the tea, are you coming down?'

There is the sound of movement upstairs, a chair moving, footsteps, a door opens with a creak and a shadowy figure appears on the landing, and descends the first few steps. Not the Virgin Mary, but a tall woman in a purple satin nightdress, a matching purple dressing gown slipping off her bony white shoulders. She pauses, surveying her audience; her timing is perfect, her expression haughty. Silver hair falls in lustrous loose waves to her shoulder blades. In one hand she trails a lavender swan's-down boa, in the other holds a lighted cigarette in a long black holder. Her gaze settles on me.

'Is that really little Elizabeth?' she says. 'My goodness how you've grown! I suppose you don't remember me, I'm your Aunty Vi.'

I am mesmerised. She doesn't look like the Virgin or a saint, but she is, without doubt, the most exotic creature I've ever seen. As I wait for her to move I can barely breathe, and strangely now, even as I write this, I find I am holding my breath. Vi completes her entrance, gliding barefoot into the room, smelling of violets, pecking my parents on the cheek and patting me on the head as we take our seats at the table. I suppose we ate tea, and I know we opened presents but even these do not claim my full attention. I have eyes only for Aunty Vi, who smokes one cigarette after another, sighs a lot and barely speaks. Everything else is a violet scented blur until hours later, as we are about to leave, Vi gets up and beckons me to follow her.

'Come with me, I have a special present for you,' she says. And I follow her up the stairs where she stops halfway to blow air kisses to Mum and Dad. 'Take care, my dears. I won't be coming down again.'

The house itself is somewhat austere, the decor in dull or dark colours; it is excessively neat, well organised, well polished, spotlessly clean, kept as though in readiness for an unexpected but important visitor. But Vi's room is Aladdin's cave; fringed lamps cast a soft light on the purple brocade chairs, the embroidered cushions, on the purple satin bedspread, and purple velvet curtains, trimmed with gold fringe. There are piles of books with tattered covers, clothes scattered across the bed and on the floor, as though their owner had just tried on and discarded a complete wardrobe, and there is a shelf of foreign dolls in national costumes. I already own two like these, one bought for me during a holiday in France last year, another in Spanish national dress, sent by a friend of Mum's who lives in Barcelona. I make for that corner of the room and stand on tiptoe to look at them, reach up to touch them. Will my present be a doll like these?

'Look,' Vi says, drawing me over to the window. 'It's starting to snow.' And we stand there in silence, Vi still smoking, watching the first few flakes dancing on the wind against the background of the darkening sky. There is a call from below; Mum and Dad are by the front door waiting to leave.

'I want you to have this,' Vi says, turning away from the window to give me a bundle wrapped in calico. 'He was very special to me, so make sure you look after him. Don't unwrap him until your daddy drives in to the tunnel.' She kisses me on both cheeks. 'Run along then,' she says. 'Have a lovely Christmas and I'll see you next year when you will be six.'

'So what did Aunty Vi give you?' Mum asks when we get to the end of the street.

I hug the bundle to my chest. 'I'm not allowed to open it until we get into the Blackwall Tunnel,' I say, rocking back and forth with impatience. I loathe the great dark entrance to the tunnel, but now I can't wait to get there. As we pass through the gatehouse, Mum turns in her seat to watch as I unroll the calico wrapping.

'Oh my God, Len, it's a dead bird! Vi's given her a dead bird.'

It is indeed a dead bird, a very large, evil-looking, stuffed parrot, dusty but intact. A parrot with amazingly realistic glass eyes and real claws, mounted on a wooden plinth, with a small metal plaque engraved with 'Hamish 1937–1943'. Hamish smells of the same violet scent as Aunty Vi. I adore him. Mum hates him with a passion, especially when he is given pride of place in my bedroom alongside the foreign dolls.

I long for our next visit, dream of being allowed back into Vi's purple room of treasures, about the possibilities of another special present: a doll perhaps, the tambourine hanging on the wall, maybe even the zebra-skin rug? The visit comes, months – almost a year – later, and I am immune to the kindness and generosity of the other aunts, waiting only for Vi's second coming. But this time Vi is 'resting', just as she is on the next visit, and the next. There is talk about her rarely appearing these days, about how she wants all her meals upstairs, about what horrors may be hidden in that room now that Aunt Olive is no longer allowed to clean it.

Vi's non-appearance was a huge disappointment on these visits. I grew angry and resentful. She appeared only once more, about three years later. The same stagey entrance, the purple nightwear, the cigarette in the same holder and this time a bunch of purple artificial violets pinned into her hair. I was enthralled but determined to punish her for her absence and pretended to ignore her, but she barely noticed me, and when she did she couldn't remember my name. I was not invited to her room, there was no special present, only the perfectly nice and appropriate ones from Olive, Gladys and Lily.

*

Years passed and I began to rail at the prospect of the long drive to London and back, the dull conversation, and having to be on my best behaviour. Even the possibility of an appearance by Vi failed to attract me. She had singled me out, made me believe I was special, then cast me aside. I usually enjoyed the company of elderly people; I was an only child living a distance away from school friends, so spent long periods with my parents and grandparents and their friends. They were all lively people who liked a party; many had travelled widely or lived and worked abroad, there were dinner parties and dances, and they were frequently heading off to London for formal dinners or the theatre. They danced and drank, and sang songs from the latest musicals, the men smoked cigars and wore dinner jackets, the women were frequently dressed to the nines in long evening dresses with matching elbow-length gloves with tiny buttons at the wrist. A lot of gin and champagne was consumed. I wanted to be like those old people, but I was scornful of the stuffy old maiden aunts, their anachronistic decor – the aspidistra, the minah bird, the piano that was never played. In my teens I rolled my eyes at the memory of Vi and the eccentricity of that chaotic, overcrowded purple room. We were a somewhat fractured family, my parents rarely mixing with other relatives, and they did not press me when I said I didn't want to trek up to London to see the aunts.

Some years later, long after I had moved out of home and was married with my first child, Mum asked me to go through the things I had left in my old room. Dad was going to paint it and turn it into a study. There were clothes, and old exercise books, some framed photographs, ancient toys and ornaments, various craft projects that I had started and abandoned, and Hamish, still wrapped in his original calico. I unwrapped him for a last look, and handed him over to Mum for the church jumble sale.

'Poor old Vi,' she said, packing him into a box with my other cast-offs. 'Oh well, they're all gone now, the maiden aunts.'

'All of them? I thought Vi was still alive.'

She shook her head. 'Good Lord, no. Vi's been dead for years. Don't you remember, when you were in Paris, we wrote and told you.'

What happened to that letter? Was it lost in the post, or was I so caught up in the excitement of living and working in Paris, of falling in love in a café on the Boulevard Haussmann, and walking hand in hand along the banks of the Seine that I simply didn't read it?

'We did think it was odd that you didn't mention it when you wrote. Vi was in a nursing home for several years, didn't know people, didn't know herself. Very sad. They're all gone now.'

I had thought of them only rarely, attended Lily's funeral, missed Olive's and Gladys's, and now they were all gone. I was appalled by my casual disrespect, my neglect of those ageing relatives who had only ever shown me kindness. I remembered the second and last time I had seen Vi, when she had actually come to the front door with the other aunts, to see us off. I knew Dad had taken a photograph of them and I asked if I could have it. When, a week or so later, he gave it to me, I propped it on a shelf and stared at it. Captured in a fraction of a second the aunts stared awkwardly back: Olive, in her floral overall, hands clasped at her waist, Gladys, her slightly crooked smile emphasised by the camera, Lily straight-faced and upright, hands behind her back and Vi, standing a little further back than the others, looking beyond the camera, the artificial violets in her hair, her cigarette dangerously close to Lil's hair. They belonged to another time, a little piece of history that I had allowed to drift away until they were gone. Olive, Violet, Gladys and Lily, spoken of always in birth order. Loathed by Alice, my paternal grandmother who had married their second brother, Len. Who were they – these maiden aunts? And what was it with the 'maiden'? Why not just aunts or great aunts?

*

The older I get the more frequently I am disappointed by the way I have let so many interesting and precious people and things, slip past me when my attention was elsewhere; fascinating snippets of history, tasty bits of family gossip, telling examples of individual eccentricity, certain people who just faded out of my life. I did not pursue those questions about the aunts when they came to me then, in my twenties, but I finally did so some years later, after reading a social history of the interwar years.

A 'maiden aunt' is defined in several dictionaries as 'an aunt who is single and no longer young', but widowed aunts are not referred to in this way. The term suggests a particular sort of redundant virginity, conjures unflattering stereotypes of lonely 'dried-up' spinsters, nosey old neighbours, harpies and harridans, all loaded with a fear and dislike of women who have lived their lives without men. In early Victorian times the maiden aunt was a favourite elderly relative who would look after the children at the drop of a hat and could be relied on for her patience, her loveable nature, endless stories, secret treats and her sense of fun. But for many women born between 1885 and 1905, the term had a different meaning and would become a fate for which they were criticised and reviled. They had grown up believing that marriage was their birthright, but the Great War changed all that. The results of the 1921 census revealed that there were almost two million unmarried women for whom the prospect of a husband and children had been destroyed. They were unflatteringly referred to as 'the surplus two million'. Many of these women made a virtue of necessity by successfully pursuing jobs and careers they might otherwise not have considered. Some started their own businesses, a significant number became writers, artists or political activists. Many simply became beloved maiden aunts, but all these women were seen as a problem, and discussions in parliament and in the newspapers of the day revealed a widespread disgust and fear of the impact of a surplus of women who would never marry. The *Daily Mail* even said 'these superfluous women are a disaster to the human race.'[1] As individuals, many of these women were loved and admired, but collectively their existence seemed to threaten the status quo.

What can it have been like in those years for women, many of whom lacked the education or the background needed to earn their own living, whose families couldn't or wouldn't support them? Many were mourning the loss of lovers or fiancés, while others mourned the loss of those they would never meet, the families they would never have. How did it feel to read those caustic denouncements that blamed them for their own misfortune? For many, the life of a single woman between the wars was a desperate and frequently fruitless search for a husband, or for acceptable, ladylike, paid work, to avoid the daily struggle to overcome the hardships of poverty and exclusion. Maiden aunts and other single women in abundance found ways to live, scrimping, saving, often going without food to maintain appearances. One maiden aunt who was in her thirties at the end of the war, turned her status into a business when her adoring nieces and nephews outgrew her care. Gertrude McLean, the seventh of nine children, established Universal Aunts, an agency to match respectable, capable women with families who lacked the services and pleasures of maiden aunts. By the early 30s, McLean, assisted by Emily Faulder, who had been her first applicant, had found suitable, pleasant and dignified employment for thousands of women who lacked professional or other qualifications. The aunts collected children from schools and stations, shopped, organised parties, picked up garments from dressmakers, acted as partners for a hand of bridge and much more. They brought joy to their charges, companionship and support to their employers, and had the satisfaction and the income to live their single lives with dignity and pride.

*

As I discovered from the fragments of family history I extracted from Dad and his brother Laurie, our family's maiden aunts each had a story, characteristic of so many of the surplus two million.

The four girls had three brothers, the birth order being: Jack, Olive, Len, Violet, Bob, Gladys and finally Lily.

By the time war was declared in 1914, their mother was worn out by childbearing and suffered bouts of pneumonia. Jack and Len had joined the army, and Olive, as the second child and oldest girl had, some years earlier, taken on the burden of caring for her ailing mother, her father and her younger siblings. Even so she had been walking out for three years with Raymond, the son of the local undertaker. Olive and Raymond got engaged the day he left for the front.

Violet had been working in a local draper's shop, but at the beginning of 1914 had got a job on the glove counter in Selfridges. There she found an admirer, the rather dashing younger son of a Knight of the Realm. Her own father was outraged by this inappropriate connection, and Edward's family would not have welcomed a shopgirl in their midst, had they known of the liaison. Vi moved out of home to live with two other sales girls somewhere in the West End, and Edward kept her well hidden, but promised that when the war was over and she was twenty-one they would marry.

Gladys, aged seventeen, and Lily almost sixteen, were both bright and rather serious girls, who helped at home and had done well at school. They wrote letters to and knitted socks for their brothers Jack and Len who were also in the army, and Bob who followed them in 1916. Gladys took some classes in shorthand and typing at the local workers club and Lily soon followed.

They were working-class people. Their father, a bricklayer, had high hopes of developing his business into a building company with the help of his sons, but that was put on hold when the boys were called up. Money was short and the family struggled to pay the fees for Gladys and Lily's secretarial training. Olive was tied to the home and Vi had moved out.

One evening in August 1916, Olive answered the front door to find Raymond's father on the doorstep. He had come to tell her that his son, her fiancé, had been killed weeks earlier on the first day of the Battle of the Somme. A devastated Olive retired to her room and locked the door for several days, emerging only to go outside to the privy. Her younger sisters stepped in to care for their mother and left trays of food outside Olive's door. A week later she came out in her best clothes to attend the small chapel service for Raymond and two other local men who had also died at the Somme, and whose bodies could not be returned. That done Olive put her overall on again and returned to her domestic role. Uncomplaining, hardworking, heartbroken all her life, she rarely spoke of her loss nor recovered from her grief. She spent the rest of her life looking after her parents and her sisters; always the one who ran the home and made it possible for the others to live their lives free of domestic responsibilities. In family photographs, except those taken at weddings and funerals, Olive is always wearing an overall, or an apron, just as she was the first day I saw her in 1949 when she would have been in her late fifties.

Vi, meanwhile, was having a good war. In Selfridges she met a photographer who was looking for models for postcard portraits, a contemporary, somewhat less sophisticated, version of the postcards of the Professional Beauties that had been so popular before the turn of the century. In those days the professional beauties were usually the mistresses of important and powerful men, one of the most admired being the actress Lily Langtry, mistress of Edward, Prince of Wales, the Earl of Shrewsbury, and Prince Louis of Battenberg. The postcards were perfectly respectable, mainly sepia or tinted head-and-shoulders shots, nothing at all suggestive, but Vi's family was shocked when she arrived flaunting her postcards. They curbed their disapproval, however, when she handed over all the money she had earned from them, to pay the outstanding bills.

The war had brought social change. When Edward was home on leave he and Vi went out on the town, dining and dancing at the Ritz and the Café Royal. Although she was still at Selfridges, she had graduated from gloves to ladies wear and had a faultless sense of style and fashion. Edward showered her with gifts and promises.

When the war ended, the prospects of marriage for Gladys and Lily were remote. According to Alice, their sister-in-law, both girls were rather plain – although I take her opinions with a pinch of salt. Gladys, who loved children and badly wanted her own, had to accept that her dream of a husband and family was likely to remain just a dream. There were simply not enough men to go round, and many of those who had returned from the war were severely disabled, or traumatised or both. Both girls were serious and hardworking and Gladys found a position in an accountancy practice where she later became the secretary to the senior partner, and to his successor when he retired. She remained with the practice all her working life, and retired in her late fifties, despite urgings by her employers to stay on for as long as she wished.

Lily had proved excellent at maths and had begun work in a bank. But as her father and brothers began to develop the building business they recognised her head for figures and for business generally, and made her a partner. She managed the office and the accounts until she too retired in her late fifties. The inky fingers that I had noticed on that first visit were a mark of her devotion to the business, which often had her working all week in the office and on weekends at the dining-room table. I never discovered whether or not the two younger sisters had men or women friends or lovers. They seem to have lived quiet, respectable, perhaps dull, but satisfying lives. Their brothers, unlike many of their contemporaries, were mindful of their sisters' situation. All three were married and eventually had homes of their own, and urged their father to remake his will in favour of their sisters. Thus they were assured of a roof over their heads for the rest of their lives. Olive, Gladys and Lily never lived anywhere else. Only Vi had broken loose and taken a risk on a different life.

Vi had expected that the end of the war would mean the start of a new life. She had met a few of Edward's friends, and expected to move fairly easily into his wider social circle. But the prospect of his family still loomed large. The war was long over and she was well into her twenties but Edward still prevaricated. It was difficult, he told her; his parents needed more time. Even so Vi remained convinced that she had a foothold on a ladder that would ensure her a place in London's high society. Perhaps Edward's original intentions had been good, or perhaps he had been lying to her from the start, but early in 1922 a friend pointed out a notice in the social pages of *The Times* announcing Edward's engagement to the daughter of a baronet. Vi's world collapsed around her.

Alice, my grandmother, a strict devotee of the Baptist chapel, always disliked the aunts, especially Vi whom she described as 'fast', and whenever her name was mentioned Nana pursed her lips in self-righteous disapproval, straightened her shoulders and sighed as if in despair. Nana had been a domestic servant – a 'tweenie' – before she married Len; so came from a slightly lower level of working class than her sisters-in-law. She insisted that Vi must have known that she would only have been introduced to those of Edward's friends who, like him, were involved with 'loose women'. His father was on the King's staff at Buckingham Palace, his mother the daughter of an even more distinguished family. He was never going to marry her.

'Vi made a fool of herself, running after him,' Nana told me, 'it was always a fool's errand. She never saw him again and she had to go back home with her tail between her legs.'

Vi did go home, but only for a few weeks, before she returned to Selfridges, and her shared flat off the Bayswater Road. I am not sure that I believe Nana's summing up; she loathed Vi, and would have wanted it all to end in the worst possible way. But Vi was determined, strong-minded, and usually got her way. So while she obviously didn't get her way with Edward, I prefer to imagine that being familiar with some of his haunts she may have confronted him somewhere, in public, and perhaps slapped his face or thrown a drink over him. I really want that for her.

Vi stayed on at Selfridges and in her shared flat, and seems to have had a few male escorts, two of them married. Only when she retired from Selfridges and moved back home to live with her sisters did she achieve respectability in Nana's eyes. It was then that Vi's world began to shrink, not simply to fit the confines of the family home, but increasingly the four walls of that extraordinary purple room, stuffed with Edward's gifts, and the trappings of the comparatively glamorous West End life she had left behind.

I was in my mid-thirties, divorced and living alone with my two sons, when I learned the stories of the maiden aunts. I had a sickening sense of disappointment that I had not allowed myself to know them better and was ashamed that I had dismissed them in the same way that the surplus women were dismissed, discounted and diminished because, in my youthful self-importance, their lives were of no interest to me. But life has a way of teaching us what we need to know and my maiden aunts, in their characteristically quiet way, have made an important contribution to my life. It was the recognition of that squandered opportunity to know Olive, Violet, Gladys and Lily that made me curious about the hidden lives of older women. I began to read stories of those lives, which then and now still fascinate me, and in my late fifties I began to write about them.

Today when I remember the aunts I recall that photograph of them proudly lined up on the doorstep to see us off, each one clad in the uniform of her life. Olive, the housekeeper, in her overall; Gladys and Lily in formal crepe day dresses, with neatly curled hair; and Vi, in her purple satin nightwear – waiting to retreat to the daily celebration of her past in the lush eccentricity of her purple room.

Blue Meat and Purple Language – Toni Jordan

Early in my mother's first pregnancy, her language began to change.
    She would have been in her early twenties then. No one knew how or why it happened, no one knew where these new words had come from. It's not that we are a posh family. We have always been a rough-around-the-edges people, sleeves rolled up and hands dirty. For some generations, our trade has been the killing of animals: we have been abattoir workers and butchers and chicken slaughterers and, in our spare time, we have kept greyhounds under our houses and, when needs be, we have dispatched them ourselves. Even our favourite ones. We are not churchgoers, but still this change in my mother's language would have come as a shock to her family. My mother left school early. She had never been one for introspection but by all reports she was mild-mannered and gentle as a girl. She didn't speak that way when she married my father, everyone agreed.
    Language has always fascinated me – the one we are born with and the ones we develop that reflect the people we become – and I love the idea of acquiring a new way of speaking, but there's a thickness in my brain that won't allow it. I'm dense at it, frankly. I've taken classes in Japanese and Indonesian and Italian and Spanish and Mandarin twice, and I've even lived in Bejing for a time, and I've failed at them all. Not one foreign word lodges safe in my head, not one single stress or construction. (This is not a familial trait: my sister is a gifted teacher and translator of Japanese.) This business of my mother's change in language all happened before I

was born so I am not a witness, but I well know the halting, inchwise progress of a new vocabulary.

At the beginning of her transformation, my mother's new words would have come out reluctantly, occasionally, in the smallest glimmers of a novel tongue. In these early stages, no one would have noticed her confidence increasing, her rapier skill sharpening, the girl turning into a woman who was not to be messed with. Neither my grandmother Muriel (in domestic service since she was fourteen, *yes Ma'am, no Ma'am*) nor my grandfather Bob (who learnt the skills of customer service in the butcher's shop) spoke that way. My mother's brother, my Uncle John, is the kindest and sweetest man I know and has stayed out of trouble from the day he got back from Vietnam. I've never heard him use one word of it. I doubt that any of this strange tongue has ever passed my father's lips, before he met my mother, or since they divorced. Not one of us bears any resemblance to her in this regard but here's the truth: my mother had quite a mouth on her.

Even among her fellow Queenslanders who could curse for England, my mother, Margaret, was gifted. She was the princess of profanity, the conquistador of the cuss. There was a balladry in the way she spoke. There was a rhythm and a meter, a weight and a measure. My mother had quite the ear for alliteration. If she was weeding the front garden and a poor struggling plant refused to yield, she would chant: *come on, you fucking futile floral fuckhead*. She showed a flair rarely seen in print and even rarer in speech. This was especially evident at the track. I can see her now, standing with her weight on one leg and her hands on her hips in front of losing dogs and bookies offering odds she deemed unfair and trainers whose dogs failed to perform as expected. She is moving her mouth as if she's chewing gum but she isn't, and she's calling them *you hopeless long-nosed brainless cunt*. At the football, she threw about the odd *you pathetic pencil-dicked waste of human skin*, even to inanimate objects like broken seats and wedged doors and fucked public phones, even to players she had never seen naked, even to female supporters of opposing teams (in particular, Collingwood). The vast majority of females are literally dickless so this curse was somewhat redundant, but she wasn't caught up in details and logic. And umpires! Don't get me started on those *motherfucking white maggots*. My mother was a performance poet at full flight, intent on capturing the spirit of the thing – but even in her small quiet moments there was rarely an *arse*-less sentence or a *prick*-free phrase or a clause missing its *bloody, fucking* adjectives.

In our family, we considered it one of her idiosyncrasies, like the way my uncle was missing several toes from playing near hot new bitumen as a toddler, or my grandmother's strange left eye, which had a mind of its own regarding direction and was always a little phlegmy first thing in the morning. When I was small, I never heard my father say one word about her language, but sometimes he would wince and flinch as though she'd raised her hand to him, even when she was talking about a mozzie or the weather or something else entirely.

My mother's is the kind of language we would call 'blue' these days, but the way she spoke always seemed purple to me: ripe and heavy as a plum, as full of meaning and subtext as a bruise. Blue is the colour of the sky and the sea and relaxation, of the eyes of calm Scandinavians and the ties of white middle-aged Tories. Common usage is clearly wrong in this regard, yet somehow, of the many definitions of purple in my fat *Macquarie Dictionary*, only one refers to language and it's this: *full of elaborate literary devices and pretentious effects*. This is what we refer to as 'purple prose', a valid and common use of the colour that derives originally from the Roman habit of stitching bits of purple fabric onto normal clothes to show off wealth and privilege, but that's not the kind of purple I mean. Our American cousins get it right. The *Collins* and the *Webster* know that another meaning of purple language is: *profane or obscene*.

It wasn't always this way. I've hunted back through newspaper archives in search of evidence of this missing use of purple, and I've found many examples.

From *The Northern Miner*, a newspaper from Charters Towers in Queensland, October 23rd, 1919, comes a report from an inquest into a shipboard mutiny. Witnesses alleged terrible conditions on board, including rotten food: 'The meat was blue on one occasion and when he complained the steward swore at him.' The title of the article was 'Blue Meat and Purple Language'.[1]

The Nepean Times, from Penrith in New South Wales, devoted a long inch-thick column on the front page to a trial for indecent language in Castlereagh on November 10th, 1928. 'The police had to repeat a rapid succession of very blanky words ... "Every second word was practically a swear word," said one witness. "It would scarcely be correct to say that language that was given in evidence ... was 'blue'. It was a much deeper shade – perhaps a dark purple."'[2]

And in another trial, this time of a man accused of stabbing his neighbour in the face, head and side with a broken bottle, reported in the *Recorder* from Port Pirie in South Australia on January 21st, 1938: 'Leighton admitted that he had about a "couple of rows a week with his wife," during which the language became "purple," and that he had smacked his wife in the face.'[3] (In this case, the swearing, smacking Leighton was the victim, not the accused. It seems that, even in the 1930s, the victim was also on trial.)

I did not grow up in Charters Towers or Penrith or Port Pirie, but I bet we would have used the word 'purple' the same way back home. We lived in Morningside, a suburb of Brisbane with the feeling of a small town in the 70s, and I sometimes sensed that women wouldn't linger on the street or at the school gate with my mother for fear they'd catch cursing like a leprous rash. It was never a question of her intent: it was unrelated to a wish to offend. I never felt embarrassed by her language. She was simply the way she was. If anyone had asked her, she would have said, *I don't know who makes up these stupid fucking rules, but I didn't vote for them so I'll speak the way I fucking well choose.*

In this, she's identified the arbitrariness of swearing, something I've always been intrigued by. It's always seemed to me that many societal taboos are more about power than righteousness. Who *did* make up these stupid fucking rules? What makes 'intercourse' more acceptable than 'fuck', and 'faeces' more acceptable than 'shit'? Is it simply an undefinable malice behind the syllables, or does it betray our deep societal inhibitions? Or perhaps it's simply a quick and shallow means of class identification: easy generalising for fun and profit, in our allegedly classless society.

The acceptability of swearing is also deeply gendered. My mother, despite her years as a successful small business–owner and single mother, was a long way from being a feminist, but the idea that certain words are not considered 'ladylike' would have made her wild. It makes me wild. In your box, ladies. Certain words, and the emotions that may or may not lie behind them, like rage or free expression, are not for the likes of you. And the fact that our most heinous term of abuse is slang for female genitals? When we open our mouths without self-censorship, humans reveal our deepest selves and our values. All of us.

That's not the end of my mother's wisdom about swearing. Despite her talent across the spectrum of profanity, *fuck* was by far her favourite. She sometimes said, *What other word has the same fucking meaning and gives the same relief as fuck? Not one, not that I fucking know of. If you slam your finger in a cupboard, do you think that saying blast or damn will make it feel better? Fuck that!*

Try it, next time you slam your finger in a cupboard. You'll find that she was right. In a study that is both elegant and hilarious, published in *NeuroReport* in 2009, researchers from Keele University in Staffordshire somehow enticed students to hold their hands in ice-water and repeat either a neutral word or an expletive of their choice. The researchers then measured their perception of pain. Not only did the swearers feel less pain, but they were able to hold their hands in the ice-water for about forty seconds longer than the prudes.

This study was not all good news though, especially for people like my mother. The researchers noted that frequent swearing dampened the effect. They surmised that, when swearwords are used more frequently, they lose their emotional intensity. It's this emotional intensity that triggers a part of the limbic system deep in the temporal lobe, called the amygdala, to initiate the fight-or-flight response that reduces sensitivity to pain.[4] For best results, then, save your cussing for when you really need it.

Now that I am a full-time writer of fiction, listening to the way people speak is a part of my job. I think I've always listened, actually. Since I was a child, this idea that my mother spoke differently from other people has sharpened my sense of the meaning behind the words, of the way that character is revealed, subtly but true, in the words that we use, the unconscious part of our expression. If I wrote a character like my mother, I'd establish her strongly at the beginning with a few sentences of her exact vocabulary, but I wouldn't continue with it. I believe in 'getting a character in' early on, hard and strong, and then removing things that will distract the reader as the piece continues. If I've done my job properly, the reader knows what that character's about. I don't need to beat it to death. Readers make suitable adjustments as they go on, and just as well, because if I were to type in every single *fuck* in every single sentence, I'd be a geriatric with RSI before I finished. If my mother was a character, for every: *For God's sake* I attribute to her, the reader would mentally substitute: *For fuck's sake*. Pop a *fuck* between every other word, and the odd *fuckkity fuck fuck*.

Still, for many people, even this truncated voice is a step too far. One thing I know from speaking to readers around the country is many readers are offended by fictional characters who swear. I'm often stopped in libraries and festivals by readers to tell me about the decline in standards, the laziness of writers, the general debasement of language and values as evidenced by swearing in fiction. As a novelist, I'm trying to replicate real life, or some altered version of it. In real life, people swear – but many people don't find this argument convincing. For some, it is instead evidence of our moral decay. We're all going to hell in a handbasket, basically.

This, of course, ignores the etymology of words like *fuck*, which likely dates from the fifteenth century. My mother always told me that fuck meant 'For Unlawful Carnal Knowledge', a sign hung about the necks of convicted adulterers as they awaited their shower of rotting fruit in the stocks, but there doesn't seem much evidence for that. The real origin seems undetermined, regardless of the enthusiastic researches of vulgarophiles the world over; this might be because the very nature of curses precluded written records, despite their prevalence in speech. Even Shakespeare, not normally considered bashful, shied away. In *The Merry Wives of Windsor*, Sir Hugh Evans is testing William on his Latin conjunctions, but himself mispronounces 'vocative' case:

> Sir Hugh Evans: What is the focative case, William?
> William: O, vocativo, O . . .
> Sir Hugh Evans: Remember, William, focative is caret.
> Mistress Quickly: And that's a good root.[5]

I'm no Shakespearean scholar so I could be reading all these entirely wrong, but this, in *Henry V*, also seems awfully close. Pistol is interrogating a captured French soldier, with the aid of an interpreter:

> French Soldier: Monsieur le Fer.
> Boy: He says his name is Master Fer.
> Pistol: Master Fer! I'll fer him, and firk him, and ferret him: discuss the same in French unto him.
> Boy: I do not know the French for fer, and ferret, and firk.[6]

Shakespeare's most famous example of copulatory description is, of course, this from *Othello*:

> Iago: I am one, sir, that comes to tell you your daughter and the Moor are now making the beast with two backs.[7]

This doesn't suit my purposes, though. Iago is being a shit all right, and trying to piss Brabantio off in the crudest way possible, but he's still describing an act rather than peppering his language with profanity. Information rather than ejaculation, as it were.

I don't feel that the recent easing of taboos about bad language reflects anything upon our moral nature other than humankind's glorious tendency to adore breaking rules. I certainly never felt that my mother's swearing reflected upon her character in any way.

Now my mother is a widow in her seventies, and I live two thousand kilometres away. She spends some of her days with her grandchildren, my niece and nephew, and she reads to them and speaks to them in plain, pure words. She sets no bad examples. Once a month she has an outing: lunch with the other white-haired women in her retirement village. By this I gather she has made friends, by this I assume she no longer speaks the way she did when she was younger, because her 'village' seems a proper place to live, and she seems surrounded by proper people. When we speak on the phone, she seems calmer. There is a new peace to her, now she has travelled most of her road. She makes me think of my favourite quote on ageing. This is Virginia Woolf, from *Mrs Dalloway*:

> The compensation of growing old ... [is] ... that the passions remain as strong as ever, but one has gained – at last! – the power which adds the supreme flavour to existence, – the power of taking hold of experience, of turning it around, slowly, in the light.[8]

That's good for my mother, of course. It's great. I'm happy for her. Imagine gaining nothing from the experience of all those years, imagine being the same raging, spouting volcano in your seventies as you were in your twenties. That would be a tragedy.

There is, however, a resignation in my mother now. It feels as though she is no longer at the height of her powers. Some of my fondest memories of her during my childhood remain the sheer vibrancy of her language and the fireworks of her eruptions. In her younger years she was utterly original, in spirit and in voice, and she showed the world who she was through the individuality of her casual utterances and the way she made people freeze and still without laying a hand upon them. In a sea of pale and beige words, she was always in technicolour. She was utterly authentic, completely natural. If there was one trait of my mother's I wish I could inherit, it was this: her lack of self-consciousness.

There was also a raw power to the way she spoke. When I was a child and there were no men in my life, I always felt safe with her, like she was armed with something visceral, like she would never be a victim. Perhaps this is why she began swearing during her first pregnancy: she was a small, thin woman protecting her baby in the best way she could. She's earned her rest, I know, but I miss the energy when her purple words went flying.

Into the Whipstick – Anne Manne

I am concentrating. I am puffing and growing red-faced with the effort of pulling my ninety-year-old mother out of my little car. Mum has grown heavier with age, and her muscles are now weak. She is trying to heave herself up out of the seat and into a standing position. Both my feet are planted firmly either side of the car door, her hands on my wrists, mine on hers. She rises, then collapses back. We start again. Foolishly, I have parked on a slight slope and her door has to open slightly up a hill. It is hard enough getting my mother out of the car on flat ground. We are weakening our effort by laughing. Finally, I winch her out.

We are standing in the middle of a great forest, called the Whipstick, in Central Victoria. It is a huge stretch of ironbark forest on flat terrain, thick scrubby bush interspersed with great tracts of ominous, dark-trunked gums, threaded with paths of ochre-coloured clay. There is no easy beauty here, except in the springtime, when suddenly the undergrowth blooms with wildflowers. I am travelling up each week from Melbourne to see my mother, after a hectic year of work. I bring her here and every time the predominant bloom changes, now yellow, or cream, or pink flowers on bushes or ground covers, spreading puffballs of colour against the dark bark of the trees. I collect Mum from the nursing home, slip in a CD playing an opera and turn it up very loud, because she is now profoundly deaf. Sometimes we pause at the lights with some lout next to us with a heavy metal beat pulsing out of his car. I turn up the volume and outdo him, and zoom off, Puccini soaring, sunlight flashing through the trees. My mother taps happily on her knees in time to the music, occasionally raising her arm in an airy, conductor's wave.

This week we have spotted a new flower, a little in the distance. The rain has made the clay bright orange and spongy, the dams and small creeks are swollen, and there are large, milky brown puddles to navigate. Mum's walking trolley sinks into the ground, leaving wheel marks. I am watching her every step as closely as one watches a toddler taking their first steps. I am anxious. The risk is that, having got her out of the car, I won't get her back into it. Or she falls and I can't get her up again, out here in the bush, miles from anywhere. Finally we get there, to the Holy Grail of wildflowers. It is a delicate, pale purple orchid. We are exultant.

Back in the car I hand her a chocolate brownie. I have discovered my mother loves sweet things after a lifetime of apparent indifference to fine food. I am afraid I throw health piety to the winds and bring her chocolates, KitKats, Tim Tams ... She polishes them off with relish – crumbs flying every which way. It has taken me a while to work out what kind of outing gives her pleasure. She is as puncturing of other people's good intentions as ever. Delicious lunches come and go without comment. With my daughter, I took her to the local art gallery to see a magnificent exhibition of Greek statues and artefacts from the British Museum. She looked hard at one of the two-thousand-year-old marble statues, with people cooing enchantment left and right. Unimpressed, she frowned and said, 'It is very ... *small*.'

When we return to the nursing home I wonder if she will remember these trips. But I dismiss it. Slowly I have learned that whether my mother remembers something is irrelevant. We all assume something like an inner camera recording experience and laying down memories is what makes an experience worthwhile. That is not really true. Long before the capacity for language or explicit memory develops, a very young child feels pleasure at a mother's embrace and the warmth and bright pricking light of a sunbeam, long before they can put a name to the sensation or can remember what happens. The *feeling* of what happens – benign, pleasurable, vibrant, or angry, cold, hard – can be enough. For an older adult losing their memory, the 'feeling of what happens' is again enough, even as they may not remember actual events. Our relation to experience can even be corrupted by the idea we must remember what happens or it is not worthwhile. And yet the consequences of good experiences are there. Without exactly being conscious of it at the time, I realise later my visits have been not only busy with practical aspects of care, but purposive in another way. I want my mother to inhabit that part of herself where she experiences being fully alive to the world. The best way, I have discovered through trial and error, is to give her music and take her out into nature. Out here in the vast, unending landscape of the Whipstick forest, there are no complaints.

If I were on an imaginary psychoanalyst's couch, doing a word association, the word which would fly out of my mouth at the prompt of the word purple would be *fidelity*.

*

The next word would be *grief*. I first really knew when she held up a standard kitchen grater that she had been using for eighty years and said, 'What *is* this?' I paused from packing away the shopping, lifting my head out of the vegetable drawer of the fridge. I was staring at it, staring at her. The world wheeled sideways and for the briefest of moments the shock made time slow. The room went dark and then came back into focus. She was still waiting for my answer. Then I mustered a frozen smile and deliberately changed my voice so it did not register the inward shock, the *'Oh no,'* and instead spoke in the rueful tone of humorous indulgence we might use for a loved one's everyday foibles. 'Mum,' I said, as if amused, *'that* is a grater.' I made light of it. But later sitting in the car I covered my face with my hands and wept, giving full recognition to the meaning of not just that moment, but all the other moments of her growing thinner and thinner before I took over meal production, of sand to repel ants spread all over the kitchen benches, of multiple phone calls and visits to sort out leaking roofs and simple maintenance, of minor car accidents and getting lost trying to find the street of her book club that she had been going to for many years. My highly intelligent mother was losing her memory.

Old age is a whole other countryside. Like small children at the beginning of the life cycle, people around an old person need to mobilise for their care and, as I have done many times in my life, I swing my full attention to my mother. In old age, however, it is more a case of un-development – of growing backwards, as one capacity after another becomes compromised, attenuated or disappears. I found myself open-mouthed, astonished, taken by surprise yet again as, one by one, an ability – to pay bills, or drive safely, or clean or clothe herself – disappeared. Long before the grater incident, I tried to stop my mother from doing much driving, especially long trips. We lived hours away from her, so I either travelled up to the country town where she lived or she came down by train to see me. The train trips have ceased. The reason is that, one day, outside the huge Southern Cross station in Melbourne, rather than wait for me to park and accompany her, she suddenly leapt out of the car, and scampered across the peak hour traffic in Flinders Street against a red light, taxis and cars skidding to a halt, honking and drivers screaming at her. At first I either drove her back or put her on the train at a small country station halfway, and someone collected her at the other end. Then even that became dicey, and from then on she could only be driven. It was like suddenly realising that a small child had acquired a new skill, and was about to squirm off the change table or climb out of a cot. One is often trailing afterwards, only what you are following is an unravelling, a movement towards unbeing, not becoming.

Like the period of life where very young children are present, work can still be done but you never know when a crisis, a fall, a stroke, or just being unable to cope with some small task, will blast it off course. I cut back on work, stop doing journalism, delay a book, and disappoint my publisher. After much discussion, my mother bravely makes an anguished decision to sell her house so she can move closer to me, to a retirement village in Melbourne. For months I travel up and down preparing her house for sale, so many times I think my tyre marks are carved indelibly into the tarmac. We are full of hope though, as if we have defiantly swung our faces to a new future, that she will have a better life. Not long after she moves, any romance about this new life vanishes. The place offers far less help than they promise in the glossy brochures, and my mother needs far more help than any of us realised.

Keeping someone completely independent when their capacity for independent living is fast evaporating is a huge operation. Bit by bit, I set up an elaborate care network. Far-flung siblings help, we roster phone calls, visits… Sometimes, cleaning up her flat, I am what the Irish feminist Kathleen Lynch calls a 'care foot soldier', but other times I am a 'care commander', and feel like a field officer deploying troops as I either give or get help for every aspect of her life. The government help is skeletal. An assessment of 'low care' means only four hours of assistance per week. It is a meaningless category, assigned when someone can merely walk to a bathroom or to a dining room. All the cosy sounding mantras of 'ageing at home', a geriatrician quips scathingly to me, really means 'ageing at your own expense'. I am more preoccupied than any time since I had young children, only now I am continually anxious, scarcely able to work, and keep compulsively making long lists of what I need to take responsibility for. They keep expanding. Banking. Stamps. Underwear. Socks. I first have to find and then pay the bills discovered in disconnected piles of paper. I make up rosters to pin on the fridge so she remembers activities each day, but worry over the indignity. Mum has got lost shopping, even in a group of residents, so I online shop and have it delivered, or bring it with me. Some fellow residents are inexpressibly kind, but others are cold and censorious, perhaps fearing a glimpse into their possible future. Another resident has put in a complaint, that Mum is dishevelled. She tells one sister pointedly that, as the village is for 'independent living', Mum should be elsewhere. We are all livid but redouble our anxious efforts to keep Mum clean. She simply doesn't notice, so as tactfully as possible I have to look through her wardrobe, find dirty items to throw in the tub. My sisters do the same. Then outfits are laid out each day between me and the council carers so she can wear fresh clothing down to morning coffee. Cleaning, medical appointments, dentists, specialists, aged care assessments … It takes hours on the phone each week just to organise it all, or to deal with local council bureaucracy to arrange meals-on-wheels, carers and cleaners. With frightening speed, even all that is not enough.

After a mild stroke and a fall which lands Mum in hospital, she is told by a kind, gruff but straight-shooting geriatrician that he doesn't think she can live independently. He asks whether she trusts me. My mother straight away answers an emphatic yes. Her trust makes it one of the worst days of my life. I feel that I have failed her. She expresses the wish to go back to her country town, where she still has strong social networks. After many weeks of searching, a whole family effort, we find her an excellent nursing home, the very best we can find.

I have been researching her medications in case they are contributing to her confusion. One has sent up a red flag. I enlist her new GP, an unusually enterprising and attentive man who does not settle for her condition being simply old age. At my request he examines afresh my mother's medications that all the GPs, geriatricians and neurologists we have consulted have okayed. He changes one that he thinks is contributing to the problems. The change seems miraculous; she is suddenly able to finish sentences and remember enough to make new friends and to start reading again. In a structured environment, Mum surprises everyone and thrives, improving in every way. She continually expresses relief at no longer having to be responsible for the things in daily life she can't manage, as the carers whisk away dirty clothing and return it freshly laundered. 'Like Magic!' she says as cups of tea and meals appear in front of her. Everyone here is in the same boat; there is loving kindness, solidarity and no judgement. She remains embedded in the family, and between all of us on almost every day someone is in contact, while old friends rally and she remains in a social network going back fifty years. Sometimes her fiercely independent spirit surfaces. When my husband and I take her out to lunch one day, she is concerned about being driven by someone she doesn't know to a funeral of an acquaintance. Mum is worried about asking for help with her walker at the other end. My husband says that maybe she look at it another way; that people might feel pride in helping her, and that there should be a pride, not loss of dignity, in asking, that she has a *right to be looked after*. The right to dependence seems, in our independence-obsessed world, a radical but absolutely just idea. Perhaps 'independent living' is idealised more than it should be.

*

On that imaginary analyst's couch, the other words which would fly out in connection with purple, would be *suffragettes*, because one of their symbols was the colour purple in garments they wore. But also *care,* because for me a feminism worth having has always included *justice* and *equality* for the vulnerable who need care and for their caregivers, but also because inequality in caregiving remains at the root of women's disadvantage. In reality, during all the years 2009 to 2015, I was struggling to do justice to my mother. If old age is a countryside, the care foot soldier's population is once again largely female. Daughters, not sons, are expected to do the care work, although there are a few exceptions. There are female carers and domestic helpers, and predominantly female care workers in aged-care facilities. I know families of several sons and one daughter, where it is the daughter who is expected to do the caring for the elderly, no matter what her profession or whether she lives interstate.

The next word which would emerge, straight after care, is *ambivalence*. In her award-winning account of early motherhood, *Maternal Encounters: The Ethics of Interruption,* Lisa Baraitser writes of how confused new mothers can be, while everyone thinks she should know what to do, and judges her closely and harshly if she does the wrong thing. Caring for an old person is very like mothering. The new 'mother' of their old parent may feel every bit as confused about the 'right' way to care. And caregivers can be ambivalent when they discover what the right 'thing' is, because it may carry with it a dilemma: the moral imperative to swing their attentiveness, time and energy toward their parents in a way that makes cherished and financially necessary work impossible. There is so much heated discussion about 'work and family' which exclusively concentrates on the so-called 'baby versus briefcase' conflict. There is much less conversation about the ambivalence and confusion loving adult children might feel on hitting their stride in a career, and being torn away by the entirely legitimate needs of a frail parent. Instead the story is told in whispers among friends or siblings, 'What I must do, what I can do, what I cannot do. Have I done enough?' And there is guilt over that ambivalence even as they act well, or guilt over the relief they feel when they arrange alternative, non-familial care, however satisfactory.

We make it up as they go along, constantly aware of cautionary tales of repellent examples of negligence and even cruelty by adult children to old parents. I hear one person say out loud she would like to take her elderly mother and dump her in another state. Several nursing home proprietors told me they had many residents who were *never* visited by any family member in all the years they had lived there. I hear a son talk of driving hours every Saturday for years, to sit in a locked dementia ward with a cruel father who had made it plain he never thought much of him. And everyone struggles with the fact that however good the alternative care, there are some aspects of a relationship which can never be commodified, where only love matters. No outside carer can ever have the shared history nor the emotional salience of an adult child. An adult child, even if they are decidedly unlovely to their elderly parent, is irreplaceable. A paid carer, even a lovely one, is replaceable.

So much has been written about maternal ambivalence. But if the colour purple reminds me of fidelity, then it must also include fidelity to the truth, and if the truth of mothering contains ambivalence towards what is asked of us, then even more so does caring for an old parent. There is much greater pleasure and joy in small children, and their becoming, and the love they give, than watching an old person disappear, their unbecoming. In dementia, as the capacity to recognise the Other disappears, so too can their capacity for sensitivity, empathy, and even love. Old age, like early motherhood, too can be shrouded in pious sentimentality. People addressing an old person raise their voices a pitch or two, sounding oh so nice, just as when they are speaking to small children. And they can register shock if the carer is resentful. Gender norms again go into overdrive. Like the Good Mother, the Good Daughter is not meant to get angry.

But adult children do get angry. Partly grief and anger are indissolubly linked, and with dementia the process of mourning a parent begins long before the moment after dying. But it is not only that. It is also an anger at how they are treated by their old parent which would be so unjust if their mother or father was in full possession of their faculties. At first, they *look* alright. Yet a moral lethargy can settle over them like a dense fog preventing sight. Melbourne writer Fran Cusworth recalls her mother's indifference to losing her small grandson at a shopping mall. She looked like the same responsible adult she had always been, but now wasn't. The elderly parent may have a huge effort directed at their wellbeing and yet not notice, querulously finding fault like a needy and resentful child. People are awfully pious, and look shocked if an adult child expresses not grief but rage at the treatment they endure as their 'loved one', as the well-meaning government brochures likes to call them, attacks them verbally or physically. Sometimes people become sweeter in nature, more expressive, perhaps like the child they once were. But they can also become nastier or more rage-filled, or express prohibited desire. Part of the unravelling is the disintegration of the frontal lobes, responsible for social inhibition. A website explains politely what to do when the 'loved one' masturbates in front of you. Or when the 'loved one' (your father) wants to have sex with you. I know some good Catholic daughters who organised a roster to sleep each night in his house to care for their father; how lovely, you are thinking, how nice, except it wasn't nice at all. The father no longer recognised them and made sexual advances to them every night. The next morning they would be up and preparing his breakfast as if nothing had happened. Other times he smeared his name in his faeces on the wall, or screamed hate at them.

All this is easier perhaps if the parent has been loving, also easier if the child is unselfish ... but what about giving care unstintingly, mobilising a whole family when the parent in question has been incapable of that kind of care themselves? Or treated their own old parents with indifference? The pleasing moral symmetry of reciprocity, the loving parent's care being repaid by a grateful child, can go seriously awry. A loving parent is neglected and ignored by an ungrateful, selfish child. Or a neglectful parent somehow manipulates children's guilt and has them flapping around him in ways he does not deserve. Frailty can make long-standing self-centredness finally justified. With small children they usually give love back in spades; a person with Alzheimer's often doesn't. Here the adult child has an enormous amount of emotional work to do, to disconnect the care they give from the treatment they get now, or the treatment they received as a child.

*

The next, rather unexpected, word my free association with the colour purple would produce, is *time*. Our relation to time changes,

Baraitser points out, in the maternal encounter. The mother is 'a subject of interruption', and as a consequence time becomes no longer linear. Time slows, becoming, she says, using a lovely word, 'viscous', thick, like treacle, slow moving. The arrow of time we follow frenetically, anxiously at work, 'becomes a dotted line, a series of segments with breaks in between'.[1] As a mother she is interrupted 'mid-sentence, mid-mouthful, mid-thought and in the middle of the night,' and there is constant stopping and starting of tasks. With the frail aged person who becomes dependent on an ethic of care on the part of family members, being 'a subject of interruption' is not so very different. A fall, a medical crisis and then another, cannot be planned for. The more hands-on the care is, as when the carer lives with someone with Alzheimer's, the more intense the experience and more similar the 'interruptedness' and parallels with 'maternal encounters', including the emergence of a new kind of self in relation to a vulnerable Other.

And just as Baraitser says, because there is so much 'stuff' to transport with infants – the bottles and nappies and wipes and prams and changes of clothes – one's relation to space changes too. The same is the case with the frail elderly. Whenever we set off, there is lots of 'stuff'. My mother's new frailty means there are hazards everywhere; once she almost falls at a small step in a cinema. The vigilance that I once needed with small children returns. I do a continual reconnaissance ahead of an outing as to where the bathrooms are and how disability friendly they are. To get to an art gallery is an expedition with pads, fluids, snacks, walking trolleys, and we need ramps and absolutely no stairs. We experience firsthand how few places cater for a disability, as even with a walker Mum can only walk half a block. We walk slowly, and stop every fifty paces or so. Sometimes she needs to sit on her trolley. Everything is done slowly.

I first really thought about cultural ideas of time forty years ago when I was sitting on my backpack on an Indian Railway station. It was long before coal-fired power stations could be seen from satellites as India underwent industrialisation. A vast network of rail providing cheap travel since the British Raj was nevertheless run in a highly inefficient way. Trains never seemed to arrive or leave on time. Once I was sitting at the station for several days. We would wait until late afternoon, go back to our hotel and then wait again the next day. Western travellers would go over to the window and an angry conversation would start while the Indian ticket vendors shrugged or suddenly could not speak English. One man in particular was in a rage of frustration the whole time, a purple vein bulging and pulsing in his forehead. He walked up and down gesticulating and speaking out loud to himself, raging at the ticket man, pacing, his neck continually craned down the line anxiously waiting for the train. At one point I chatted to him, thinking he might be missing out on a meeting with a beloved in far-off Mumbai. He wasn't. He was just going to another holiday destination on a yearlong overland trip to Europe. He actually had all the time in the world.

It was an encounter with a different time zone, determined by culture. We forget in the West the astonishing change in our consciousness demanded by industrial time, deadlines, set working hours, lives no longer set by seasons, of light and darkness, of harvest and fallow. Western travellers responded to the vagaries of the railway in different ways. I would slip into a writer's reverie and scribble in my notebook, lost to the world around me. In truth? I was quite happy, and I admit that sometimes I was rather peeved when an ancient locomotive finally sputtered into view because it meant breaking up ideas that were flowing, sudden action, packing away my pencil and notebook, rushing to get a top bunk, and a window that opened.

Returning home I never felt quite the same about time. I began reading about how the working class and children were integrated into the discipline of industrial time, the factory sirens, the school bells, the endless measurement and disciplining of their relation to time. Submission did not come without struggle. My metaphor of the Indian Railway often sustained me during childrearing, where plans are routinely capsized and nothing seems to arrive, career-wise, on time. You get there, I told myself, just like on Indian Railway, in the end, even if not on time. And there is a lot of pleasure along the way.

But I was younger, and time seemed an infinite expanse stretching out ahead of me. Now I have lived far more years than I have left so my relation with time is less dreamy. Moreover, a writer's life is full of deadlines, which last year were especially pressing as I had a new book out. It now takes me a little while, and no little moral effort, to relax and get inside the Slow Zone of Care. When I come to see my mother, a game of cards at first seems interminable. I find it hard not to check emails on my iPhone. Sure enough when I finally succumb and sneak a look, there are all kinds of work obligations, interviews or request to give talks I should immediately attend to. I pause shuffling the deck of cards and send messages back to my publicist with a satisfying sound of a whoosh like a rushing wind, as if to emphasise the speed of the device I am holding. But this device also traps me: I am expected to respond at once, in a mere millisecond, to never be away from work, an expectation of instantaneity. As I spend more time here, slowness gets easier and easier, and more enjoyable, just as it did on Indian Railway. The book tour is finally over and the imperatives of work slide into a fuzzier focus, they are no longer in sharp, hard outline.

Our relation to time is deeply hierarchical, and shaped by culture. Time is a status marker; anyone giving time to others is usually lower in social status. There is a subtle or not so subtle downgrading of anyone in the Slow Lane. Time is also deeply gendered in a way that is quite simple, with a profound, long-lasting impact on women. Women's time is still meant to be available to others, for care, with what's left over devoted to paid work. Men's time is meant to be made available for paid work, with what's left over available for family. The assumption is they are a care commander who has a female care foot soldier doing all the care work. 'Good' women are marked by their willingness to give time. Women have traditionally acted as time sentries and time wardens, preventing intrusions into men's time as wives, secretaries and assistants, and as conservers of the family time bank, able to be drawn on as needed. 'Don't Disturb Daddy' is the name Susie Orbach and Luise Eichenbaum gave the phenomenon of tiptoeing around men's time.[2] Women's time in contrast, seems porous, a door that is always open. Care of the aged still carries an assumption that a woman, this time a daughter, is not at work, has all the time in the world to attend to her old parents.

Even the oft-used word, 'spent', to describe time passing, is not innocent of its impact on how we see care. It shows not only the irrevocability of time which has gone, but of new, exploitative attitudes to time; that it *ought* to be about *productivity*, and *efficiency*, all the opposite values of any ethic of care of the frail aged, especially someone who is losing any sense of the straightness of Time's Arrow. 'Spend' also carries inflections of the domineering relation of the business world, of 'time is money', of males at the top of the hierarchy whose attitudes to care go unchallenged. 'I am too busy and too important to "waste" time on care.'

*

And yet ... my last word on my analyst's couch connected to purple would be *courage*. 'Old age is not for sissies,' says one of Mum's friends, quoting Bette Davis. I am often silenced by my mother's courage. I don't want to sentimentalise this period in her life, but her matter-of-fact braveness is one reason why none of this is simply burdensome. As Baraitser says, an 'encumbered experience is in an odd way generative'. How did an unencumbered life, so remote from most people's experience, with such vasty unequal consequences, ever become an ideal? All this time spent with my mother is deeply valuable to both of us. Certain ghosts in the mother knot have been laid to rest. Sometimes I have struggled to get here, but our time together can be quite lovely. My mother is more expressive of affection than at any other time in her life. I find new sources of respect for her, or perhaps rediscover them. I am moved by my mother's gritty stoicism, her adaptability, her uncomplaining resilience. Especially I admire, how in spite of everything, she goes, full of joy, into the Whipstick.

Velvet – Rachel Robertson

1

It is rich, deep purple velvet. Even now, it pulls you to touch it, to feel the silken allure. Cut into a rectangle with pinking shears and stuck onto a piece of buff card, it can fit into a woman's palm. On the back, the words: 'a bit of coronation robe.'

We found this, my sister and I, upstairs at my mother's house in a box file that contained things from her childhood – old photos, a menu from her parents' wedding, and her birth notice. The words on the back of the card with the purple velvet are in my mother's handwriting. My sister's grey eyes darken as she holds it.

We are captured, both of us, by these mementos from our mother's past, most of all by the sample of purple velvet, symbol of another place and time.

'Yes, my father gave me this,' says my mother, though she doesn't remember when.

Because she is eighty-seven, my mother thinks it is time to pass on the contents of this box. She decides to loan it to me so that I can photocopy the material for my siblings. That day I leave her house cradling the precious cargo of her past in my arms.

She knows I am the writer in the family, the memoirist. Did she think about this when she passed the box to me? Does that mean she trusts me to write about her past or not to do so?

I am the memoirist in the family but the one with the worst memory. I often have to ask my siblings about events from our childhood because they seem to remember more than me, even the youngest. It's an embarrassing irony, but I wonder if this is perhaps *why* I write memoir. To try to piece together a past that is hazy and unreliable, to make the self more real.

But how do you write a life when you have only fragments?

2

'That piece of purple coronation robe – roughly when do you think your father gave it to you?' I ask my mother on my next visit. She is unsure but she knows it was before the war. After some discussion, we decide that this piece of material must be from King George VI's coronation in May 1937.

'I remember watching the Princesses in the Royal Jubilee celebrations,' my mother says. 'I was about eight. My father's office was on St Paul's Churchyard and his office was on the ground floor, but the firm above his gave us seats at their windows to watch the procession.' My mother is one year younger than Queen Elizabeth.

'But that wasn't a coronation,' I say.

'No, I suppose not.' She looks a bit vague. She's had a long and full life. Some things have gone from her memory, others are anchored there firmly. I can understand her remembering the Jubilee: it was a major event in London and because of her closeness in age to Elizabeth she would have had a particular interest.

The Silver Jubilee of King George V was in 1935, so my mother would indeed have been eight. She would have had a good view as the royal family approached St Paul's Cathedral where a Thanksgiving service was held on 6 May 1935. There is an image on the St Paul's website of a painting by Frank Owen Salisbury called *Reception of King George V and Queen Mary at the West Door of St Paul's Cathedral, Jubilee Day*.[1] Queen Mary is so pale she looks like a waxwork. Behind the King, Prince Edward looks both supercilious and ill-at-ease (one reads the future into such works) while the princesses Elizabeth and Margaret are dressed alike in pale peach outfits and hats. Behind them stands a Sikh in full regalia. Judging from the existing film of the event, I would say this painting is a work of imagination rather than documentation. And memory, too, is part imagination, each memory a recreation rather than a reproduction.

3

The image appeared to me when I was reading *A History of Silence* by Lloyd Jones. Something in the texture of the writing summoned a form into the back of my mind. I put the book aside for a moment and allowed the shape to grow, and there it was, a pattern of lilac and purple petals, a texture that was almost velvet – was it velveteen perhaps? The design was a version of paisley. I could stroke it down my side, so it was a dress. Like a mini jigsaw puzzle of memory, it slotted together and I could see and feel once again my first special dress of purple velveteen. A dress that made *me* special: in this dress I shone, for a moment I was centre of the picture, no longer just a spectator.

Imagine this, plain shy Rachel clothed in such a dress!

Immediately, I feel a need to verify this image. I wonder if my memory of the colours and design is correct. It was the 60s, so bright colours and patterns were in vogue, as was velveteen. Mainly, though, I got my older sisters' hand-me-downs, so my clothes were at least ten years out of date. I often wore matching outfits with my younger sister, both outfits having been originally worn by my two older sisters. Sometimes the clothes were exactly the same (there was a pair of Chinese-style pink blouses I remember, which we always wore with green skirts and homemade hair bands of the same green) but other times the styles were the same but in different colours. In principle, I had no problem with wearing matching outfits with my little sister but in practice I could see that she was more attractive than me – cuter, funnier, prettier, more confident – and that it did me no favours. I wasn't resentful of this because I adored my little sister but I was self-conscious about it.

I'm quite sure that the purple velveteen dress was an original. It was made or bought just for me and there was no matching dress for my sister. This might have been one of the reasons it was special to me. Recreated now in my mind, I see it is also a beautiful piece of fabric – the balance of white, lilac, deep purple, black and lime green, the warm and the cold colours combined, the way the design is both soft and spiky, with its stylised leaf shape.

I'm suddenly struck by the fact that the living room and kitchen in my house are decorated in white, black, purple and lime green. I don't even like the colour lime.

4

We use memories as a way of forgetting. What we remember allows us to forget other events and therefore create a coherent life story.

But what if the forgotten comes to us, like a dream, a tear in the fabric of our life?

5

I am twenty years old and wearing a lilac t-shirt, a white skirt with a broderie anglais frill and my new purple suede sandals. I have painted my toenails purple to match the sandals. I sit in a chair in my flat and a man kneels before me. Earlier, there has been a fight on the stairwell of the apartments across the way and I have watched anxiously from my balcony. The man strokes my thighs. He takes off my sandals, slowly, caressing me with his velvet voice and his eloquent hands.

'I like your matching toes and shoes,' he says, smiling in such a way that I don't know whether or not he is laughing at me for wearing purple nail polish. He pulls me to my feet and we walk upstairs to my bedroom, where he smiles again in the same and different ways.

6

'Did you see any of King George's coronation, then, when you were ten?' I ask my mother. 'Maybe you saw them on their way to Westminster Abbey.'

'I'm not sure, dear,' she replies.

I show her some internet photos of King George VI in his coronation robe, which does indeed look very similar to the piece of purple velvet she has had all these years.

I know very little about my mother's father, only that he was a textile merchant in London and died when I was three years old.

'How did your father get this bit of the coronation gown?' I ask my mother. She doesn't know. Possibly it was my grandfather who supplied the purple velvet himself to the royal dressmakers. I think this is unlikely as I'm sure someone in the family would have mentioned this before now. We aren't monarchists but it's the sort of thing that would have been discussed. We decide that her father must have known the merchant who supplied the material to the dressmakers. As a textile trader himself, he would have known other traders. I can imagine a friend giving him a sample of velvet from the roll that the King's Imperial gown was made and him passing it to his daughter as a keepsake. It must have been a potent symbol to a self-made man whose parents migrated to London from Eastern Europe before he was born and who grew up in the East End.

7

At my mother's house I go upstairs and look at her row of photo albums until I find the right one – dated 1963 to 1973. It is years since I've looked at this album. In fact, I can't even remember when I last opened it. The first pictures of me are grainy black-and-white photos of a baby wrapped in a shawl. Soon I am a toddler and then a little girl. Many of these are in colour, and quite a few of them are badly faded, blotched or discoloured. It makes me feel I'm viewing an artefact in a museum.

I look for the purple paisley dress. I look through every page of this album and then through the next one (1973 to 1985). There is no purple dress. When I think about it, if there had been a photo of me in this dress then I probably wouldn't have forgotten it for over forty years. It's a disappointment not to see the dress, but looking through the photos is surprising. I see that, in fact, my little sister and I were very similar as children and that both of us look sweet in the photos. Perhaps she is slightly prettier, but often it would be hard to tell us apart except that I am older and taller than her. Our matching dresses are smart, too, and suit us. They don't look at all like hand-me-downs. There are photos of me in several very pretty, obviously new, dresses – a cornflower-blue dress, a red and white pinafore, a chocolate-brown dress with a very smart belt – that are later handed down to my little sister. It's true that I am more likely than my siblings to look self-conscious in the photos or turn away slightly but, actually, there are many good photos of me. It seems strange to recognise this after remembering myself for all these years as the plain one in the family, wearing other people's cast-offs.

As for my purple dress, I'm now beginning to doubt myself. Is it confabulation, borne from a desire to have been, just once, someone special? It's not hard to invent memories and rewrite your past. A writer, especially, is often tempted to fill in forgotten details and then may wonder if their imagination is functioning partly as memory anyhow.

As Drusilla Modjeska has noted, imagination and evidence vie for ascendancy in memoir, and memoir itself, she suggests, is as much 'a mapping of a mind' as the recreation of experience.[2] The purple paisley dress is now part of my family story whether it actually existed or not.

8

A small parcel comes for me, postmarked Cambridge. It is from my oldest sister and she has sent something just for me. I am eight years old and this is the first time I remember her being away from home. Inside the parcel is small card with an Arthur Rackham illustration of Alice in Wonderland and a lilac silk handkerchief. It is the finest handkerchief I have seen. It is so soft and smooth and the colour is like the foxgloves that grow in our garden. Does this mean my sister hasn't forgotten me?

9

I am having dinner with friends in an outside courtyard. Pink bougainvillea grows up the walls and some of the flowers lie on the ground, faded to a dusky pale purple.

'Look,' says my friend to me, 'your shoes match the fallen blossoms perfectly!'

It is at this point that I remember that other moment, thirty years earlier, when I wore purple sandals and nail polish. It's as if I had lost the memory of that evening until now, because, although I have thought about the man and my relationship with him quite often in the intervening years, I have never before remembered that evening of the fight, the way he took off my sandals, the mixing of his laughter and desire, my anxiety and desire.

Richard Holmes says, 'There is a goddess of Memory, Mnemosyne; but none of Forgetting. Yet there should be, as they are twin sisters, twin powers, and walk on either side of us, disputing for sovereignty over us and who we are, all the way until death.'[3] I believe that Mnemosyne was the mother of the nine Muses and so I like to think that Calliope (the Muse presiding over eloquence and epic poetry) in particular would have been close to her troublesome Aunt Forgetting.

10

On winter evenings, my sisters and I undress in bed, tossing our day clothes onto the floor and pulling on our brushed-cotton nighties under the sheets. My older sister taught me this trick – not the oldest (the one who went to Cambridge) but the next one, still six years older than me. If we can, we do the reverse in the morning, staying in the warmth of the bed until we have some haphazard layers upon us. The three of us share a bedroom but we are sent up to bed one at a time, based on our age. My little sister (she of the grey eyes) is quite often still awake when I arrive for the night and so we talk quietly until she falls asleep, sometimes in the middle of a sentence. Some nights we can't sleep and I climb into her bed and write words on her back with my finger and she tries to guess what I write. This, too, is a pastime started by my middle sister and passed down.

After my sister drops off, I return to my own bed, making that cold hop between them as fast as I can. Then I create a cave under the covers and read by the light of a small torch. I think my parents know I read late into the night but it is a quiet, 'intelligent' thing to do and therefore acceptable. Much less acceptable to my mother is the addiction I have to pulling out tufts of wool from my pink candlewick bedspread. It is a delicious feeling as the wool pops out, and the spaces left behind are marvellously blank. I seem unable to resist doing this. Sometimes I pull out a whole section, and then the flower that was once there disappears completely, leaving no trace except emptiness. It is like undoing the past.

11

Undoing the past, too, is what the memoir writer does as she creates her narrative. Memoir asks: what is the shape of a life? And in answering that question, the memoirist reforms the past as she creates her patterning. Like the fabric maker, she weaves her warp and weft, assembling her artefact. If she doesn't like the look of it, she can unravel and recreate it. If I wanted to, I could completely wipe out the story of the man who saw my purple sandals, or change it so that he seemed less ambivalent about me and I more fulfilled by my experiences with him. I could perhaps turn my purple toenails into a powerful statement of confidence and passion. But

I avoid this temptation because memoir, to me, is not just about remembrance and reflection but also about mourning.

12

In London, I tell my cousins about the purple velvet scrap and ask if they know anything about our grandfather's business. They know very little more than me. It seems that after serving in World War I, my grandfather took a job as an office boy in a firm of textile merchants who dealt in silk and woollens. Before long, he worked his way up the firm, developing new designs and adding colours. He was one of the first London traders to turn to artificial silk or rayon and to screen-printing rayons. According to my family, he was 'rather a Fabian' and felt that not only rich people should have coloured prints to wear. He also supplied parachute material for the troops during World War II. One of my cousins shows me a sepia photograph of my grandfather, his five brothers and their mother. The men are all dressed in suits with white flowers in their lapels and the mother, who was blind by that time, is dressed in a long dark dress. No one now remembers the occasion of this photo.

All life stories are fragmentary but it seems wrong that the pieces passed on may be arbitrary. Lloyd Jones writes, 'Foundations come in all forms – texture, language, heritage, entitlement. Some things are buffed to be remembered while other things fall away.'[4] We may never know what things have fallen away or why.

There are things we don't tell others, that we keep silent with us to the grave. They may be a dark secret but often I think they are just small things, moments we want to hold close and never share, thoughts that come in the night but melt away by day, events that no longer hold any energy, that seem to have happened to someone else. We live many lives in one lifespan; so, too, our memories can seem to belong to a previous self.

13

The man who admired my purple sandals disappeared from my life. Later – many years later – he returned for a brief moment to ask forgiveness. His voice was still silky and rich, his hands now silent.

14

Where my mother has trouble remembering the past, my son has trouble forgetting. Not only does he remember many more dates and phone numbers and facts than most people, he also remembers people's exact words, even years later. If I say, 'Remember how you used to cry when it rained?' he will reply, 'Yes, and on the fourth of April two thousand and five you said to me, "It rains on the just and the unjust," because you were annoyed that I was upset about the rain.' Or if I say, 'It's a long time since we've been at this part of the river for a swim', he might say, 'Yes, Mum, we were here on a Sunday last January and we saw dolphins and I had a chocolate ice cream,' and he will probably remember how many times and when we have been in this place over the past few years.

His mind is so full of facts and words that sometimes he can bring nothing useful to the fore. If he remembered less, he might find navigating each day easier. It is as if his autobiographical memory seems to work differently from mine and many other people's. Most of us, in remembering the events and feelings of our life, remember first times and unique times. We are interested in specific events only in so far as they contribute to meaning and a comprehensive story of the self that puts us at centre stage. For my son, other events and facts may be equally important to those that place him at the centre of his own story. This makes our discussions about the past very interesting, because he remembers quite different things from me and I find myself reviewing my take on earlier events we have shared. This is going to be a godsend when I'm my mother's age!

Interestingly, both failing to remember and failing to forget make imagining the future difficult. We use our memories to make decisions about the present and shape a projection of our future. A blank past creates a blank future and an over-cluttered past seems to have a similar effect.

If 'memories always have a future in mind',[5] I wonder what my son's limited forgetting suggests about his vision of his future.

15

The purple paisley dress from the 60s sits in my mind as a memory. The image is very clear, and carries with it a strong emotional charge of mourning. If autobiographical remembering is 'mental time travel' as Tulving suggests,[6] then this feeling could be a response to the loss of the past – imagined or otherwise – or the loss of forgetting. For something may be forgotten for good reason – what we would call repression or denial. Adam Phillips notes, 'There is haunting and there is discarding; and it is not always within our gift to decide which is which.'[7] Once discarded, now it haunts.

I could ask my sisters if they remember this dress (I'm sure my brother wouldn't), but what if none of them do remember it? Maybe I would have to delete this fragment from my story. What then would replace this particular haunting?

16

My mother is the last of her generation, just as my father was for his family. Like many of my generation, I wish now I'd asked her more when she was younger. There would have been silences and gaps – there is always the forgotten and the untold – but perhaps I would have gained a better sense of her and her parents' lives. Soon, there will be no more tales. All we will have is our own faulty recollections and the family photo albums with their slanted stories.

17

Over the years, I seem to have collected many purple items – cushions, vases, clothes, jewellery and glassware. My brother made me two purple anodised steel speakers with jazzy purple covers. My sisters have regularly given me purple scarves and candles and personal items, the most recent being a stripey purple and black watch made of recycled 1930s bakelite.

Purple, of course, is well known for its royal connection. But I have also read that purple is the colour of ambivalence (that combination of hot red and cool blue), of creativity, and of mourning. To me, purple is pure pleasure. And it seems right that pleasure may also encompass ambivalence, imagined and forgotten stories, and loss.

'Is a Magnificent Story': Interviews with Pigeon Fanciers – Sarah Drummond

At the pinnacle of Mount Waychinicup lie several gnamma holes the size of bathtubs, carved into weathered granite by symbiotic relationships between weather and people. My friend and I were there, where granite boulders bigger than blocks of flats squatted among alpine gardens and stunted forests of marri. I knelt beside one of the holes and peered into the water. Tadpoles and strange beetles I'd never seen before swam around.

I was thirsty. I put my hand into the water and just before I'd scooped it into my mouth I saw the feathers, circling in flotillas over the water's skin. Tiny and iridescent purple, the feathers gleamed like an oil slick in a roadside puddle. The feathers changed my mind about drinking from the pool. Then the sight of a bird's wing bones lying on the bottom confirmed it. A yellow glass bead glinted beside the bones.

The peak is so isolated and difficult to get to that the only signs of humanity are ancient ones. And there lay a glass bead. In a pond. Tiny, shining feathers on the water's surface. I reached down to the bottom of the pool and picked up the bead.

The feathers, the bones and the bead. 'It's a pigeon's leg ring!'

I had visions of this doomed pigeon crashing into the mountain in an exhausted daze – or maybe it was killed by a raptor and taken to the peak to be eaten?

That night in the cave, we lit a fire and cooked some kangaroo meat with garlic and mushrooms. As the sun set, the lakes and creeks sitting in the country below shone in the low light. We squatted in the dirt by the fire and inspected the leg ring with our headlamps. Then we got out our smart phones and started googling 'Danriz. Loft #5'.

Now you may think that googling a dead racing pigeon from a cave nestled into the top of a mountain is unusual, but it was quite sedate compared to the mother lode of pigeon fanciers we encountered on the internet that night. A YouTube clip, posted by the owner of our unfortunate pigeon, depicted his avian heroes posing coyly among graphics of sparkling rainbow fireworks and red love hearts, to the strains of that ultimate stalker song 'Every Breath You Take' by The Police. I recognised the purple feathers cloaking the birds' throats. Seeing those feathers set to the music completely did my head in. The clip was unsettling but I kept returning to it like a dysfunctional lover. I wanted to understand such single-minded adoration, even fanaticism, for a *pigeon*.

Over the next few days we explored the mountain and the one next to it, joined by a saddle of prickly hakea forest. We found a nineteenth-century sealers' camp, the remains of a less-ancient marijuana crop, a white cross in a cave, close to the site where several narcotics detectives and the local whale spotter pilot had crashed in his Cessna in the 1990s. We became lost in the damp, mushroomy karri forest late at night and ... well, all these things are another story. The whole time, I kept the pigeon's leg ring in the coin pocket of my jeans. On returning to civilisation, I searched out the dead pigeon's owner on the internet and rang 'Danriz'.

'Hello, I'm Sarah. You probably don't know me. Um, I think I may have found one of your pigeons. Do you live in Albany? Do you have pigeons?'

'Ah, yes, yes. You find my pigeon? Where you find my pigeon?'

'At the top of the mountain, at Waychinicup.'

'The mountain? At the top?'

'Yes. At the top. I'm sorry. I didn't find a live pigeon. I found feathers and bones of a bird and a leg ring, in a pond.'

'Ahh, the peregrines ...' he sighed. 'What number?'

'Number? I don't know. Loft Five?'
'No, no. The blue ring.'
'I only found a yellow ring.'
'Oh, okay.'
'You might know me. I used to sell fish at the Sunday markets.'

His accent sounded Filipino and his name Dante echoed the impossibly romantic and deadly histories of Spanish conquistadors. The local Filipino community were great patrons of our stall. They liked to buy whole, fresh fish (and a fishmonger who has to fillet for hours on a Saturday appreciates a customer who prefers whole fish on a Sunday).

'Fish? Not pigeon?' Dante sounded confused. 'You want to sell me fish?'

'No. No! I want to give you the pigeon's leg ring. I'll drop it off tomorrow if you like. Where do you live?'

Later that night, Dante sent me a text message: 'Ah ok ako lang pala nakapag pauwi sa 1000km sa.wa. sikat ibon natin' which I translated rather clumsily as, 'Ah, okay homewards now SA 1000km. SA to WA. Famous bird.'

Dante arrived home with his wife and children, as I parked on his verge the next day. He was a short, sturdy man with bushy eyebrows that made him look stern. In the YouTube clip he was wearing a short straw hat, Chilean style, but this day he was hatless and his hair was speckled with white. A Jack Russell rabbited around our feet. Dante showed me into the backyard, to the pigeon loft.

 'Three weeks ago, the club take three hundred birds to Laverton. One hundred birds came home.'

'You lost two hundred birds?'

'Yes, yes. The peregrines. They eat them. They eat only brains,' he picked at his head with his fingers. 'Only brains.'

Two hundred pigeon brains.

'How far is that? How long?'

'They fly eight hundred and sixty-five kilometres. We set them at eight in the morning and the first three come home at six o'clock.'

'I couldn't drive from Laverton to Albany in that time.'

'Yes. Very fast. We have big races in Adelaide. This bird, this is a famous bird,' he pointed one out to me. The pigeon eyed me. A fine looking bird, sleek and muscular, its beautiful purple throat reminding me of the gnamma hole at the top of the mountain.

'All over Australia, people come to race birds in Adelaide. We send them when they are babies. November thirtieth. Then July we race them from Marla or Coober Pedy, one thousand kilometres to Adelaide. That bird is a famous bird. He came –' he holds up two fingers.

'Second?'

'Yes. Three thousand dollars prize.'

I have to say that at this point I was dangerously close to becoming a pigeon fancier. I'd entered the murky world of a subculture previously beyond my ken. I was beginning to understand the theme song to his YouTube clip. Stalker song? I think not! *Oh, can't you see, you belong to me* is really about the relationship between a man and his homing pigeon.

'Can you tell me the name of the club president?' I asked Dante.

Dante put me in contact with an old man who knew a thing or two about racing pigeons. Days later, Ray and I sat in the sun outside his house. He was eighty-seven and had been in bed all week with the flu, so he was appreciating the warm air.

'You want to know about pigeons?' He handed me a book. 'This is the best bloody book I ever read, mate. Got everything in it. Here, take it.'

'They say I have a way with birds and animals,' he said. 'But specially birds. I've been racing birds for seventy years now. Since I was little. That'll open your eyes, hey?' We talked pigeons for a little while. He told me about his pigeon lung, a common pigeon fancier's affliction. He talked of how young people weren't interested in racing, how well the races used to be attended and not so much anymore. I followed him up the hill to his hutches where pigeons sat on the roofs, gleaming, iridescent, eyeing me cautiously.

'But I can tell you another story if you want to listen. It's all in here.' He stabbed with his fingers at his West Coast Eagles beanie. 'Have you ever heard of the Kalgoorlie race riots?'

'No … I don't think so.'

'Nineteen thirty-four, mate. Bloody race riots. I was there. I remember it. It's all in here.'

There was an intensity to his words. I thought, my goodness, these pigeon racers are fanatics. *Race riots?* Did these guys really riot over their pigeons? In 1934?

'Let's go and sit down,' I said. 'Do you mind if I record your story?'

'Nah, nah, mate. I'm happy to talk. You can tape whatever you like.'

The recording, because I couldn't work out how to do a voice recording on my phone in the seconds I had before he started talking, is a ten-minute video of a pigeon fancier's sock in a black plastic sandal. This next piece is transcribed verbatim.

'In Kalgoorlie about that time, they reckon they were doing slingbacks, you know? To make a bit of money on the side?'

'Who? The pigeon owners?'

'Nah mate! The Italians. And the Aussies. Anyway. That's only half the story. This day … er, the bloke's name was Jordan. And the Ding's name was Mataboni, he was the one who owned the –'

'Was that Maroni?'

'Nah, Mataboni.'

'Okay.'

'He threw this bloke Jordan out of his pub, you know? But when he hit the ground, he was stone dead. And some stupid bastard yells out, "He's got a knife!" but Mataboni didn't have a knife at all but anyway, the game was on.'

'So the Australian man was dead?' I had realised by then that this story wasn't about pigeons.

'Yeah. But anyway, it was one of the best sporting families

in Kalgoorlie, the Jordans. The game was on. So this Saturday morning, six or eight o'clock, a bloke, an Aussie bloke, he come to our place, said to my mum, "We're gonna give the Dings the run around tonight, Mum." You know ... lucky for me I got it all in here. And that night it was on, mate. The Aussies burnt all their hotels down. We were kids. I remember it all. Then they burnt all their houses down. All their shops down. Ah ha. Then anyway. There was a copper there and he's taking all the kids' names, you know? He couldn't stop them, a lot of bloody maniacs, anyway, this is true. They were going along saying, "This one's a good Ding", "This one's a bastard, we'll burn his house down", this is true. So they came to this house and this Slav is standing in front of his house trying to protect his family and the bastards shot him dead, see?'

Ray shook his head. 'My old mate, he said, "You can't do that," he said. He said that. They were his exact words. He said, "I don't mind burning his house but I don't wanna shoot no poor bastard." They were the exact words he used to me. But he died years ago, so I'm using them myself now, see.

'You may think it's bullshit but it's not bullshit, mate. This is the truth ... but anyway ... two days burning houses down and a bloke called Joe who had more testosterone than bloody brains, so all the Dings were down by the railway line building trenches to save themselves, dug themselves in and this bloke got his mates together and they pulled all these pickets off the fences and used them to charge them, they charged them just like in the war with bayonets. It's true!'

'That was nineteen thirty ...?'

'Nineteen thirty-four.'

'Was that the same year as the Kristallnacht? You know, the night of the breaking glass, with the Nazis ...?'

'Nah, nah that was a few years later.'

'Oh. Okay.'

'Yeah well. There was other blokes see? Good blokes. My father was a violent man. You wouldn't know it from looking at me but he was. Oh, but he was a violent bastard. Anyway, so that night, he got his twenty-two out the bloody corner behind the kitchen door and a packet of cartridges out the cupboard, I can see it now. Like it was the other night. I didn't know he was gonna go out and find this Ding though and bring the poor bastard home, see? His best mate from up on the mine. So he brings him home and hides him under his bed for two days and two nights. I didn't even know he was there. Two days he hid him. I'll bet that'd open your eyes, hey?

'I tell you what, the people who were there, there's no one left alive now. My mates are all dead. One of my mates said afterwards, "You couldn't find any young men between sixteen and twenty in Kal after that. They'd all bolted!"'

'Right. So you reckon men between sixteen and twenty were the ones who were burning and –'

'Oh yeah. All over the world, it's the same age, no bloody brains ...' He laughed then and I could see the tension of the story leave him for a moment. 'I was six, you see? Six. And I can remember that bloke saying to my mum, "We're gonna give those Dings some hurry up tonight, Mum."

'There was another bloke too. Everyone reckoned he was getting slingbacks from the Dings so they burnt his house down too that night. And while they were burning his house down, he was trying to put it out with his garden hose and someone chopped off his hose with a bloody axe. That's the truth. But of course it goes back a lot further than that. Hoover, the bastard. He sacked all the Aussies from the mines and kept the Dings and Slavs on. Bloody well cut their wages and increased their hours! It'd been bothering the Aussies for a long, long time. Twenty years. You know how that is?'

'Mmm. Yeah, I get that ... hang on, hang on: Hoover?'

'Yep, took off and became president of the United States, didn't he. Left all that bloody trouble behind. Jesus Christ, that's the truth. It'd open your bloody eyes, eh?'

He finished up at this point, took off his glasses, wiped his eyes and put his glasses back on. I turned off the recorder.

Then he said, 'You know, two days later me and my mum were looking out the front window at these Italian women walking down the road, in the middle of the road they were, with wheelbarrows full of tents and cooking pots and clothes and water bottles and things. Those women's faces were as black as the clothes they wore ... from the soot, you know, from sorting through their burnt out houses. Me and Mum was watching the women, and I remember her crying. Mum had tears streaming down her cheeks.'

None the wiser about the Great Southern pigeon racing fraternity that day, I drove home with Ray's book about pigeons and some rather chaotic thoughts. Kalgoorlie Race Riots? Hoover? Pigeon lung? I kept thinking about those homeless women walking with all their worldly possessions, *their faces as black as the clothes they wore*, to the outskirts of Kalgoorlie where they set up a refugee camp by themselves.

*

Not long after talking to Ray, I was to have an unexpected interview with a third pigeon fancier, during a trip to Bali.

In a small room off Hanoman Street, Ubud, the tattooist pauses his needle from my foot and looks at me.

'You alright, sista?'

I nod but he had already felt my leg twitching as his gun hit nerves and pressure points. I am sweating, lost in a strange world of low-level, insistent pain.

'We have a quick break,' he says.

It's early evening. The noise and heat is intense. Scooters, jeeps and taxis beep and roar by, ferrying people between the day and the night. Street-side, the tattooist smokes, his bare hands streaked in the powdered flock from his plastic gloves. His little brother comes to sit with us on the bench, waves his fist at his leonine dog to squat on the concrete at his feet.

'*Selemat mallam, guark*,' says the little brother, looking at the outline of a crow on my foot.

'Good evening, crow?' I ask him. 'Is that what you say?'

'Yes, *guark*, a crow,' he smiles. He is softer, younger than his brother. 'I like birds.'

'What is your best bird?'

'Pigeon. I have plenty of pigeons.'

'You have pigeons? Do you race them?'

He looks confused.

I say, 'You know ... ah ... competition?'

'Ahh, yes! All around Bali. Very fast birds. When I was little –' he holds his hand a metre above the ground, 'I have lots of pigeons. My mother say, "Take birds away! Too many pigeons!" So I took them to the market and sold all the pigeons. The next day, they all come home!'

'Ha! Homing pigeons. So you had money *and* pigeons!'

'Yes!' He laughs. 'Now, I have fifteen pigeons. I sell them every week at the market. Sometimes they do not come back but most times, I get my pigeon back and I sell them again.'

'That's so cheeky! Don't you get pigeon buyer come to your house with big stick?'

He shakes his head. 'Another man sell them for me.'

His brother, smoking, watching the street with the kind of detached cool that only tattooists possess, stubs out his cigarette in the bakelite ashtray and nods me inside.

*

It seems that I am now the proud owner of a book about pigeons.

I rang Ray a few weeks after he'd told me the story of the Kalgoorlie race riots. I begged him for a longer loan of his book because I hadn't finished reading it yet. Also I'd promised him a copy of my own book, *Salt Story*, in return for his allowing me to interview him.

'Keep the pigeon book for as long as you like,' he said on the telephone. 'I've been a bit sick anyway. Been in hospital. Had a minor heart attack apparently. That'll open yer bloody eyes, won't it!'

'Sorry to hear that, Ray. I won't stay long. I'll just knock on the door and drop off my book.'

'Nah, mate. It's too cold for me to go out today. Just put the book on the back veranda for me.'

The weather was rancid that day and it started hailing as I drove to Ray's house. I parked in the driveway and hunched around through the chill to the back of the house, past brightly painted concrete gnomes, potted geraniums and cast-iron garden chairs. I left my book, wrapped in a plastic shopping bag, under the veranda clothesline. The plastic sandals he'd worn the last time I'd seen him lay beside the doormat, the imprint of his feet pressed into them.

Five days later, his death notice was in the local paper.

Ray had told me that he was the last person alive who had witnessed the Kalgoorlie race riots. I'm not sure if he was right about that, but I reckon he'd be close. His passing away, he being a man with whom I'd had a cursory but... what is the word... instructive?... enlightening? conversation with just once, reminded me of those pigeons who were given medals after World War I, for carrying one small but vital story strapped to their bodies. Ray wasn't a loved one to me. We'd not even shared a cup of tea but he told me that story because he wanted someone to remember it.

I rang the president of the Albany Pigeon Racing Association and told him of how I'd first encountered Dante and then Ray.

'Oh yeah, we lost a lot of birds that day,' said Ed, referring to the club's two hundred pigeons that didn't make it home from the Laverton race.

He was a tough talker and his speech cadence reminded me of the racehorse trainers from my adolescence. But he was also keen to emphasise the humanitarian aspects of pigeon racing. 'It breaks our hearts to lose so many birds. It really does.' I knew that it only takes a single piece of footage of cruelty or negligence to go viral on the internet, and that he was carefully selecting the information he gave to me.

'You know when you were camping and found Dante's loft number on the internet?'

'Yes.'

'Well, sixty years ago you would have been receiving pigeons with messages, Sarah. The thing is, what we are doing looks like a silly old hobby, but when the world goes back to bows and arrows, when everything breaks down ... well, we lost a lot of birds that day but we have to press on. We have to maintain the old knowledge and not lose it. We have to press on because one day, you never know, hey? One day pigeons may be the fastest way of communication that we have. Again. It's really important that we continue.'

His dystopian vision both amused and impressed me. It struck me that whenever I started talking pigeons with strangers, some kind of witchery occurred. Stories occurred, retellings that hardened into narratives over the years. Stories about stories even. We harbour stories; they are strapped to us in the same way as pigeon fanciers strap stories to their birds' legs. As soon as people realise you are listening, they will unfurl a tale and hand it to you. It's just the way it is.

'I will tell the club this story,' said Dante, the day after I'd returned from finding purple feathers floating in a gnamma hole at the peak of Mount Waychinicup. 'That woman who climb the mountain and find my bird. Is a magnificent story.'

With thanks to Dante Salvadore, Ed Shilling, the tattooist's brother at Bali Bagus Tattoo, and Ray Barrass (dec.) for sharing their stories with me.

Do You See What I See? – Tracy Farr

The American Modernist artist Ad Reinhardt wrote in his 1957 manifesto that 'colours are an aspect of appearance, so only of the surface'.[1] Reinhardt left colour behind from that point, and painted only in shades of black. 'There is,' he wrote, 'something wrong, irresponsible and mindless about colour, something impossible to control'.[2]

For twenty-odd years I worked as a scientist. Writing scientific papers – responsibly, mindfully – could sometimes feel like painting only in shades of black. Perhaps that's why I turned to fiction: to let control and responsibility slip. I write fiction not only from my own lived experience, but from what I imagine the experience of others – real or invented – might be. Rather than mindlessness, it's a case of putting myself in the mind of another. I listen with their ears, dress in their clothes. But it's not just appearance and surface: I see what they see. And what I see is in sharp focus, and full, blazing technicolour.

*

My first published fiction was a very short story called 'The Sound of One Man Dying'. In just five hundred words the main character, Gwen, reviews her own life and struggles to comprehend death after the loss of her husband.

> Gwen had been trying for some months to hear the sound of Alan's death. To smell it, to taste it, to see it. She had thought the colour for it was yellow, for a time, early on. His mother

had been disturbed ... when Gwen wore the old yellow bridesmaid dress to his funeral ... [Gwen] had decided within days after the funeral, though, that Alan's death had deepened to dark purple.[3]

That story's clashing flash of yellow deepening to purple (like a bruise unmaking itself) is evidence that among my obsessions in fiction is colour, and its ability not just to signify, but also to disturb. My interest in colour is part of a broader interest in sight and perception, and many of my short stories concern themselves centrally and specifically with sight: with visual arts, with ways of seeing, and with sight's loss.

The nameless first-person narrator of my short story 'The Blind Astronomer' is not me, although she is like me in some aspects. She works as a scientist, as I did when I wrote the story; her aunt, like mine, is an artist. Her description of herself could be me, describing myself:

> I have a love of colour, in clothing, hair and nail colour, favouring bright, clashing colours, choosing them for the ways the juxtaposing colours assault my eyes. Peacock blue with clashing pink, blue and green should never be seen, stripes with florals, hair dyed flame red, fingernails painted the colour of spring grass. Aunt told me I dressed like a blind woman, not meaning it as the compliment for which I took it.[4]

In the story, the narrator skips out of the astronomy conference she's attending, to go drinking. It's that particular type of drinking and general misbehaving that happens at conferences (the scientific conferences that I went to, at least).

> I slipped away early with some like-minded friends, and we headed from the hotel bar to a rib joint downtown to a student bar by the river to I don't know where. I woke up with my

head resting on the toilet seat in my hotel bathroom, and left Minneapolis later that day with a hangover that lasted all the long way home to New Zealand.[5]

That two-day hangover was mine in real life. But the real-life conference – in the northern hemisphere summer of 1993 – had plant biology, not astronomy, as its subject; and home for me, then, was Vancouver, not the New Zealand of the story. Our boozy real-life night ended up, after that 'student bar by the river', at First Avenue, the Minneapolis nightclub made famous by Prince – the Purple One – and the setting of much of his 1984 film *Purple Rain*.

Life fuels fiction; fiction holds truths that sit, waiting to resurface – waiting for an invitation to *write about purple* – and to connect.

*

I take colour – its beauty, what it adds to my view of the world – as a given, a constant, as fundamental. But how constant is it? Does purple for you look the same as purple for me? And when I say *purple*, do I mean the same as you do, when you say *purple*? That's the question that preoccupies me: do you see what I see?

At the heart of that question lies this: what is colour?

For us, now, in the twenty-first century, the physical properties of colour are well documented; hue, saturation, and brightness are objective, quantifiable, measurable. But still, our interaction with colour is essentially psychological: colour is an attribute of experience, 'a construction of mind'.[6]

Isaac Newton recognised that colour is not a property of things but is generated by the eye and mind: 'Rays ... have no Colour. In them, there is nothing else than a certain power and disposition to stir up a sensation of this Colour or that'.[7] Newton sought to understand colour by measuring light, by separating the objective, quantifiable, mechanical behaviour of light from the subjective experience of it. He split light through a prism, shone it onto a wall and observed the colour spectrum it made. Then he remade white light by bringing the colours together.

By Newton's reckoning, the spectrum held seven colours, all in a line from red through orange, yellow, green, blue and indigo to purple/violet. In his *Opticks*, Newton took that line of seven colours and curved it around to form a colour circle.[8] To form that circle he had, in a sense, to disregard the physics: in Newton's colour circle, short-wavelength-purple was no longer *distant from* long-wavelength-red; it became, instead, *adjacent to* it. Continuity and contiguity were created – beyond quantifiable, mechanical, objective sense – because the colour circle made perfect, intuitive, aesthetic and perceptual sense. It makes sense to us still, for purple to nestle between red and blue, to connect them.

*

I learned the rainbow's colours by the science-class mnemonic ('Think of it as a name, Roy G. Biv.') and so I see those seven colours when I look at a rainbow; the mnemonic itself forces their seeing, even if I cannot tell quite where to draw the line between orange and red, or blue and indigo. The Ancient Greeks saw only three colours in a rainbow: purple, yellow and red. Newton devised a seven-colour circle, while other theorists proposed stars, rays, spheres, tables and wheels as colour systems, with or without names, numbers or other codes to define each colour. Different colour systems have proposed (or enforced) symmetry, or emphasised asymmetry. All these models aimed to control or quantify colour objectively, to 'articulate a coherent colour system',[9] but their differences only serve to indicate just how subjective colour is. Colour is not *within* a thing itself, but is in our perception of it: in eye, and mind; and, particularly, in language.

*

Colour is only ever crudely mapped by words. A common theory of language evolution describes the simplest state, the most isolated societies, as using just two terms to encompass all colours: some version of 'black' and 'white' (or dark and light, or cool and warm). Red is added as the first 'true' colour; only over time are other colours named. It's not, of course, that we don't see or distinguish those colours we have no names for, but simply that 'the colours we can name are lodged in our memory in a way that others are not. Nameable colours are the beacons by which we navigate colour space.'[10]

Writer and critic A. S. Byatt has described the names of colours as being 'at the edge between where language fails and where it's at its most powerful'. Referring to historical, regional and linguistic differences and specificities of colour words ('*green* and *yellow* in Ancient Rome probably meant *blue*'; '*purple* in French always means *red*'), she concludes that the interest to a writer is in knowing that:

> [readers] will have very quick physical reactions to [colour] words, and some of them will immediately see what you see, and some of them will see quite some other thing, and some of them almost won't see anything. And this can lead you philosophically to think about the fact that really, truly no reader reads the same text as another reader.[11]

The notion of *purple* – of what that word means (and its changes in meaning) through time and culture – offers an example of the depth and range, but also the slipperiness, of colour language. In the Ancient World, purple obtained from shellfish (*Murex* and others) was the most highly valued dyestuff. But lustre and glow were more important than hue (colour) in defining purple; even the very cost and preciousness defined a thing as *purple*. A dichotomous dark–

light property of shellfish purple was much admired: 'though it seems to be dark, it gains a peculiar beauty from the sun and is infused with the brilliancy of the sun's warmth'.[12] The best purple-red cloth was described as looking 'dark by reflected light, but a fiery-red by transmitted light'.[13] In later times '*purpura* was ... the name of a silk fabric, not a colour ... we find many "purples", from white and yellow to blue and black, as well as red and green'.[14]

The Ancient Greek idea of colour (*chroma*) was related to skin (*chros*) – the surface or appearance of a thing – but also to movement and change.[15] Reflecting this, the most important colour-technology of the Ancient World – producing *Murex* purple – was multi-stage and complex, itself a process of transformation, development and change, producing a sequence of colours from yellow, yellow–green, green, blue–green, blue and red, to violet.[16]

Colour sequence and transformation also characterised alchemy, which sought to transmute unstable substances into stable substances (lead to gold, say) in a process marked by colour change in a particular sequence, perhaps black to white to yellow to violet.[17] Isaac Newton's own alchemical notebook referred to the 'peacock's tail' stage of the alchemical process – the shimmering iridescent surface of heating metal.[18] The peacock was frequently depicted in early Christian textiles and mosaics as a symbol of immortality, shedding and renewing its tail-feathers each year, but in alchemy, the peacock came to symbolise the notion of everything in one, the one containing many: the whole array of peacock colours emerges from a single white egg.[19] More specifically than that general symbolism of all in one, though, it's an embodiment of the presence of all colours in white, the peacock-tail spectrum of light fanning out, via the prism, from egg-white light. When Newton – scientist, philosopher, alchemist – named the colour spectrum in seven steps, he not only made it in the likeness of the musical scale,[20] he also drew alchemical connections. His conception of the presence of all colours in white light owes much to the peacock.

*

There are peacocks in that story of mine, 'The Blind Astronomer'. The narrator – the astronomer – dresses in 'peacock blue with clashing pink'.[21] Later, she sees a peacock's tail feather on a railway track, odd and out of context, disturbing:

> The sun's dying light hit the track, showing a milky streak curved across four of the railway ties, like the spine of a big fish picked clean by eager teeth ... it was a peacock's straggly tail feather, its eye eaten away, or maybe just tucked ... out of sight ... Aunt once told me that peacock feathers are bad luck. But I've always and only seen their beauty ... a universe unfolding into colour and movement ... how could those hundred shimmering eyes be anything but lucky?[22]

That story is full of eyes. There's the 'artist's eye' that the narrator employs, seeing the beauty in her science: 'I've seen the planets with an artist's eye, charted their courses with a sense of ... beauty ... It is a gift Aunt has given me'. But many more of the story's eyes are flawed: the peacock's feather with 'its eye eaten away'; the childhood operation to correct vision; a mark on a photograph that 'scratched out' eyes; even the disembodiment implied when the narrator remarks on resemblance, 'She had my Aunt's eyes'.[23]

Flawed eyes and different ways of seeing provide insights about colour and vision, the brain and perception, light and physics. The effects of eye-defects (including temporary abnormalities, ageing, and drugs) can be seen or surmised in art. Rembrandt greatly reduced the number of pigments he used in old age, restricting his palette. The shape of a long-beaked bird appears in the later works of Edvard Munch, painted while he was suffering from vitreous opacities that disrupted his field of vision. J. M. W. Turner's eyesight was failing with age and illness when he painted the glorious hazy light and steam of 'Rain, Steam and Speed', the purple–orange sky of 'The Fighting Temeraire'. The question remains whether the changing palettes and techniques of artists suffering from vision defects resulted from that blunted vision, or from artistic intent.[24]

Recording of visual phenomena was often first made by artists. Painter Philippe de La Hire reported from his studio in 1685, 'The light which illuminates hues changes them considerably; blue appears green by candlelight and yellow appears white; blue appears white by weak daylight, as at the beginning of the night'.[25] It was not until 1866 that the mechanisms for this phenomenon, whereby changes in light level affect how we see colours, were distinguished and described by scientists: rod cells were adapted for seeing in poor light, while cone cells operated in daylight.[26] The physical properties of objects do not change as the light illuminating them changes, but our perception of their colour does.

Colour, in the end, comes back to our perception of it; in synaesthesia, perception is complex. Margaret Visser describes synaesthesia as 'the mixing of senses so that taste (say) gives rise to geometrical images, hearing is coloured, shapes sing'.[27] The two most common types of synaesthesia are colour-hearing (*audition colorée*), particularly musical colour-hearing; and the association of verbal sounds, particularly vowel sounds, with colours.[28] The artist and synaesthete Wassily Kandinsky, reviewing synaesthetic experiments in his 1912 book *On the Spiritual in Art*, wrote:

> [their effects] would seem to be a sort of echo of resonance, as in the case of musical instruments, which without themselves being touched, vibrate in sympathy with another instrument being played. Such highly sensitive people are like good, much played violins, which vibrate in all their parts and fibres at every touch of the bow.[29]

Synaesthesia circles us back to that first short story of mine. That story starts with synaesthesia, with colour and sense: 'Synaesthetes smell music, know numbers by their distinctive colours, letters by music'. Like Gwen, the widow in the story, I can't 'claim that degree of sensitivity, that consistency of sensory overlap',[30] but synaesthesia has always fascinated me. Margaret Visser, herself a synaesthete, notes that 'synaesthesia shares a few characteristics with the phenomenon of perfect pitch'.[31]

*

With my own far-from-perfect pitch, I've found myself singing two songs while I've been thinking about, researching, and writing this essay. They've come to me, these songs, for their textual connections, and they've stuck around, in that odd, earwormy way, the whole time I've been writing. One song I've sung for its title, that titles this piece. In Hunters and Collectors' 'Do You See What I See?'[32] the chorus repeats its title in a call and echoed response – 'Do you see what I see?/DO YOU SEE WHAT I SEE?' – the response insistent, demanding, shouted, as if with caps lock engaged. I hear it in its broadest sense, encompassing the ideas I had in mind to write about here: colour, light, perception, different ways of seeing.

The second phrase I've been singing, over and over, is the chorus from a Paul Kelly song, 'I'd Rather Go Blind',[33] and this is more specific in its relevance. Paul Kelly might prefer blindness to heartbreak, but I can imagine few things worse than losing my sight.

*

It's twenty years since my mother lost her sight. She was in her early fifties then, the same age that I am now. My mother still has some peripheral vision, but has lost her central vision. In 'The Blind Astronomer' I used an analogy my mother uses to describe her sight loss:

> *Like having a clenched fist held in front of each eye* is the way they like to describe the vision I'll retain. Why bother just

holding those fists there, I want to tell them, why not just punch my lights out and be damned. The horror of it.[34]

As I type this, I can see my mother do the movements to demonstrate: clenching her fists, holding them in front of her eyes, as if to mime exaggerated crying, *boohoo*.

My mother's condition has a similar effect, but with different cause, to macular degeneration, 'robbing … sight entirely, from the centre out'.[35] The artist Georgia O'Keeffe was eighty-four years old when she lost her central vision to macular degeneration. O'Keeffe is in 'The Blind Astronomer', too; the story's epigraph quotes her: 'My first memory is of the brightness of light, light all around'.[36] I used my own experience for the story's O'Keeffe elements: I saw the O'Keeffe exhibition at the Minneapolis Institute of Art that the story's narrator sees, and I posted to my husband the postcard photo of O'Keeffe that the story's narrator posts to her aunt:

> The photograph showed O'Keeffe in the desert, the hot sky white around her, O'Keeffe glaring directly at the camera. Her trousers were black, her shirt white. She surrounded a bleached cow's skull, stark against the black of her trousers. Georgia's eyes stared out at me from the image, wide and unblinking, black as uncooked beans.[37]

My postcard was delivered, as was the narrator's, with a scratch across Georgia O'Keeffe's eyes.

> A solid patch on the picture side was scratched out, perhaps by some sharp-edged sorting machine. There was a perfect, even rectangle where the thin laminate of printed paper had been etched from the photograph, leaving the blank, rough, white card exposed. The scratch covered – obscured, exactly – her eyes. They'd scratched out Georgia's eyes.[38]

My real-life scratched black-and-white postcard prompted the astronomer's fictional one, as my real-life hangover prompted hers. Georgia O'Keeffe never fails to trigger in me memories of summery Minneapolis and drunken nights, to a soundtrack of *Purple Rain*. Black and white and purple all over, life fuels fiction, the connections impossible to control.

*

Just recently I discovered a delightful – if dead wrong – citation of 'The Blind Astronomer' as an essay, in a 2010 paper, 'E-Accessible Astronomy Resources', about making databases and other online resources more accessible for 'physically challenged' astronomers. The paper discusses results from a study carried out at the University of Helsinki (2005–2009), and concludes with this paragraph, quoting my fiction as fact:

> Practically everyone who lives long enough has to face physical challenges at some point. An astronomer who is able-bodied today could have accessibility issues tomorrow. We cannot expect that she or he is willing to give up practicing science. In her essay *The Blind Astronomer* (Farr 2002), the New Zealand astronomer Tracy Farr eloquently describes the changes brought by the gradual loss of her vision. With a different approach to looking at the research data, she can continue to access the universe:
>
> > 'I am freeing myself from the fixedness of the seen. With my mind open to the universe, I hear the heavens' ebb and flow as music. It is the incomprehensibly wonderful revelation of music first heard after only ever having seen black spots and lines on a white page. As my ears open and my eyes close, I hear the planets dance.'[39]

What strikes me most when I re-read 'The Blind Astronomer' now, though, comes immediately before those four sentences that Isaksson quotes:

> ... in comparison to the fixed film of seen memory, the image not seen is loose at the edges, its elements mobile and interchangeable. It holds the promise of universality.[40]

I know that my mother no longer sees what I see. She has lost precision and detail from her vision, with images 'loose at the edges'. When she reads, now, she must read audio books ('ears open ... eyes close'). She can no longer see faces. She's had the guts (the centre, the heart, the eyes) punched out of her sight. I imagine this dark centre as unknowable, painted in shades of black. She is left with peripheral vision, though, and, because I can't bear not to, I romanticise – I invent and imagine (I fictionalise) – what she sees. I conjure a corona of glorious colour, its elements mobile, ever-changing: egg-white light split through a prism, a peacock-tail all-in-one shimmer, sea-green, *Murex* lustre, bridesmaid-dress-yellow, a bruise unpurpling. With those rose-coloured glasses firmly in place, life unfocused holds the promise of universality; it is blurred, but bright and beautiful.

Mary – Lucy Dougan

for Larry, and for Sophie

Lovely as they are, things lose infinitely from being preserved not used.
Virginia Woolf, *Diaries*[1]

It's not a failure of imagination: think of Helpston as a village in a wooden box, thatched cottages, church, public house, cows, sheep, and enough figures to dress the set ... Johns and Marys, all of them. The chain stretches back ...
Iain Sinclair, *Edge of the Orison*[2]

Distaff (*n.*) a tool used in spinning; the female branch or side of a family; a woman's work or domain

Faces

At the hinge of spring and summer, the suburbs of Perth are a purple carpet. As barefoot kids we were always warned about the bees that might be hiding in this fallen profusion. Between those small bells, and the pavement lines, and the prickles, there was a lot of hopping about, a lot of staccato skipping. Our first child was born at jacaranda time. I remember the profundity of crossing the border from a single state to owning a body that had made another. The nurses came and drew a face on my chart – happy – sad – in-between? Mine always smiled. I understood that they were busy and had their systems, their checks, but at times I wanted to howl *I am not fucking happy*. This life-changing thing has happened to me and I am feeling any combination of bliss, pride, fear, sadness, awe, etc., all rolled into one. But happiness, no. In the early evenings

I would walk our baby to a big bank of windows at old St John's and we would both look out to the jacarandas as far as the eye could see. I'd tell him this would always be his time of year, his estate, this purple slide to summer.

*

We think, perhaps, that it is the ones to be born who are waiting, but it is our ancestors too. They reside now in the digital sea. Some are surprised to find themselves recycled in merchandise or in museums. On the radio a commentator says we are not close to them anymore, that we are living in a long, continuous hiccupping present of compressed, homogenised culture, but I think that is not always true. It has taken me years to walk back to Mary or for her to walk forwards to me, but at a two generation's remove on my maternal side she does not feel distant in the least. Once, with old photos splayed about everywhere, a friend snatched up one and said *oh my god that's scary, she has your serious face on, the one you use when you talk about art.* I think I shrugged – *normal, why not, to look like an ancestor, surely*? But now I would say what is the matter with that, with looking serious … even at the risk of an imposed smiley face.

Perhaps sometimes Mary's expressions do inhabit mine and I am happy to think that they do. But she gave me much more than that too.

*

In the house into which I was born there was an under-the-house. My childhood room, a long narrow sleep-out, perched above this underground. One summer, my mother dragged an old brown trunk from the darkness. Then, I knew nothing about the house, how it had come into the family, who owned it and so forth. It was simply home, named *Cathay,* with its large wild garden, shingled roof and strange room configurations that had been modelled on a sea-captain's ship. It lay in a line of houses that I thought of as my mother's, my grandmother's, my aunt's. Or rather, they were the figures that I most associated with those houses even though my father and my uncle were around.

When I asked my mother what was in the trunk she said *maybe the other life of the house*. We found tatty papers, abandoned knitting, infant shoes and then the mask that my mother snatched up quickly. It was a face made of linen with eye-holes and a mouth. We took turns in it, running crazily around the garden, but there was already something about the mask that made me wary, some itch or inexplicable periphery that it announced. Breathless, I asked my mother who had made it. *Probably my nanna*, was all she said.

Oh, I replied.

That night I thought about the countless times I had fallen asleep, unaware of the mask in the trunk in the under-the-house in the room beneath my bed. Was there another room again beneath the under-the-house? How deep did things go down? And how many faces had been left there by how many old mothers for me to try on?

*

In the crypt there are not only people's things. And what is added to the store is endlessly unfinished, overlapping, changeable.[3]

Cloth

As the baby, the youngest on both sides (all sides), I have always lived with a strong salvation narrative. Keep the family together – no matter – at what cost, yes, all of those platitudes. Contrarily, my sense of family is strong; my sense of family is fragile. I imagine this is not unusual. We try to stay close. We try to hold it together. Sometimes it works. Sometimes it doesn't. I am a half to my five brothers and sisters. I am no blood relation at all to my oldest first cousin, Axel. I can still picture his wry expression over the kitchen bench from me on his last visit. *Look at us – the oldest and youngest – and neither of us really Dougans*. It's only later that I remember the napkin with the cursive 'A' embroidered on the corner. A is for ...? I cannot locate an 'A'. Is it a stray from my husband's side with its Anthonys? And then in flash I know it is 'A' for Axel. It is an inclusive 'A' stitched by someone in the family for a German child arriving by postwar boat to a strange country, to a whole future he is yet to own. Old linen can spark off a detective bent. Who, who, I ask my mother, in all this family, can have got this napkin ready for Axel? She thinks for a bit. *If she'd been alive then, I would say Mary.*

*

She was a great sewer. More than that, a professional seamstress. She sewed for society women in Melbourne in the last decades of the nineteenth century. She sewed matching outfits for my mother and my aunt when they were children: for the Royal Show, pale blue dresses with Peter Pan collars and flared skirts, for the opening of the family-owned Regal Cinema, crushed velvet evening coats. When my mother was older, Mary copied Vivien Leigh's dress from *Waterloo Bridge* for her, soft crepe, rose-pink with a taffeta slip.

In old photos young Mary is a figure of great elegance with her wasp waist and piled up curls. The clothes she wore she would have made herself: high-collared blouses with puffed sleeves, long tailored skirts in taffeta and other cloth depending on the season.

And she came down to us through the words for cloth that are now unused – serge, cambric, sateen, twill – words that are folded and packed away these days in special glossaries, words that are folded and packed away like the material she left in the houses of my grandmother and my mother. A great floating dowry of cloth for now unmade garments. A box, a chest, above/below ground, an endowment, an estate.

Somewhere in our present house is something that Mary had begun and set aside. It is indeterminate. Maybe the lining of a dressing gown, maybe the beginnings of an evening dress? It's a mid-purple silk with Chinese embroidery of a slightly darker colour, a kind of silky damask. I try to know where things are, to hold onto them, but often I lose track. On some days, in this Age of Curation, I am happy that things slide out of my grasp. On other days I am appalled.

*

Purple is also the colour of bruises (life holding on too hard), the wet violets at Mundijong, the sheen on dark feathers, an eye-shadow compact I owned called Wuthering Heights, decomposition.

The Long Awaited

When did Mary come to me? Or when is it that I needed her? It was in that hinterland of starting and stopping bleeding – the 'painters and decorators' in/out, out/in – a buffeting. The residue in public toilets of other women's menses would bring tears to my eyes. It was pathetic in the truest sense. I needed something, someone to get me over this hump. I started to notice older women as if truly for the first time: their dress and habits, their survival tactics, their public kindnesses to one another. Once I bumped into an older woman with my shopping basket at the supermarket and apologised. She turned and grasped my free hand with her own that was piled with rings. *You don't have to say sorry.*

*

There is a list of disjointed facts that I know about Mary Coade (nee Tindale).

She was the second daughter of 'the Bolter', Margaret Thompson. I guess every family tree has one or two. In *Love In A Cold Climate* the character is simply referred to as *Bolter*. Being *esposito*, I am rather fond of economical reasons being given for mysterious origins. My paternal grandfather, with his heavy Irish accent, always said *Ach, dere was an impediment*. In a trajectory from Ireland to Newcastle-on-Tyne and then on to New Zealand, Margaret married her employer, Robert Tindale. They moved as family, Margaret, Robert, Mary and her elder sister Bess, first to Victoria and then to Western Australia where Robert set up the Perth Modelling Works.

Mary met Ted Coade in a shop in Victoria. They shared a birthday. Someone had called out to greet one or the other of them with a congratulations for the day and they both answered. It is thought that the gold rush may have brought them west.

Later they would run a haberdashery business in Newcastle Street, Perth. Renee, a daughter, came along quite quickly. Ted managed the social aspects of the shop and Mary, the finances. Through her shrewd management, business expanded. They bought farms in the Wheatbelt and opened other businesses around Corrigin and Wickepin. Tom Hewett, a building contractor recently returned from World War I, met Renee Coade in Wickepin where she was living with her parents and working as the postmistress. They were later married and had two daughters: Dorothy in 1923 and my mother Lesley in 1925. Ted and his son-in-law Tom, my maternal grandfather, would eventually co-own and run *Lambton Downs*, the Wickepin farm on which my mother and her sister lived idyllically until mid-childhood. It was this country, this particular place, and the people in it, that were to shape Dorothy Hewett's work for a lifetime.

My mother remembers her maternal grandparents, Ted and Mary, as loving, hard working and unpretentious. In her recollections they are already old and set in various routines. Ted played billiards with Tom every Sunday night. Mary came over to Renee and Tom's every afternoon and sat on the sofa. On Friday nights they went to the Regal. They summered in an old weatherboard place at Como with a retainer called App. Ted loved the garden at *Cathay* and kept it up. Mary practised her Christian Science lying on the bed at the farm with her lessons, having 'the right thought' for those she felt in need, the tracts printed on pale pink and mauve paper. When Ted died and Mary's memory was failing she would ask the family for her husband. The answer, *He's just in the garden*, satisfied her.

*

There is a sculpture by Patricia Piccinini called *The Long Awaited*. A preppy young boy who looks like he might have walked out of a Spielberg movie cradles the head of an ancient woman whose bulky body morphs into a tail. It recalls that branch of work on early peoples which held to the idea of marine origins. She is no svelte sea nymph but solid as a dugong. When I stand in front of it I think of Mary and all of the ways that she walked towards me, or I back to her.

She came to me through that sea of material. She came to me through my mother's stories. She came to me through the upside down plaster brick in the café near my work with the words Perth Modelling Works carved into it in beautiful Gill Sans. Sometimes to see a woman's story it is best to look upside down, arse about etc. And she came to me through a newspaper clipping that one of my colleagues showed me. It announced the estate she left her daughter Renee, the estate that would trickle down to my mother, my aunt, and finally to my sister, my cousins and me.

A friend clutched my hand beneath the upside-down Perth Modelling Works brick and said, much like the song in the movie, *You must follow this!* But it was not explicitly or only pecuniary, this estate. It was also the estate of 'may I' versus 'can I'. It was the estate of great wild gardens and physical freedoms, a mother who could only bear to hit you through an eiderdown. It was an estate of places belonging to three women in a row – safe places you could skip to, one from the other, spaces that held their own particular light and dark, aromas, domestic routines – beloved as the house in *Howards End* or the lady house in *Lolly Willowes*. And ghosting these abodes, always that expansive childhood lived on farms with largely indulgent adults, at least for most of the time.

The Big Row

There is a poem of Dorothy's about the big row.[4] Why wouldn't there be? For years after the girls, my mother and aunt, went to bed and prayed that there would not be another row like it: *please dear jesus make the quarrel stop*. It was a row over 'can I leave the table' versus 'may I leave the table'. It was a row between grandparents and parents of the worst kind. *Let her do as she likes. No, not until she says 'may I'*. But my aunt left the table anyway, causing in my mother's mind, the baby sister, an indelible sense that some form of excessive rebelliousness had been practised and that nothing would ever be the same again. And perhaps she was right. A may/can scenario sounds like the worst kind of petit-bourgeois hairsplitting, hardly worth a fuss, but it must have been (or became) emblematic of a deeper rift, a recognition or acknowledgement of my aunt's difference and a signal to her that it was okay, or even encouraged, to begin on a path of defiance. How many grandparents are complicit in exactly this? Many no doubt. After years of playing hard corners with their own children, they are free to get subversive with the next generation. Now, I think of the family bolshiness, particularly in the female line, all being anchored back to that may I/can I split. And I think of Mary's resourcefulness, her creativity and everything it gifted to her descendants, female and male. There's a poem about that too:

> nobody said   *You're girls*
> *You can't do these things*
> So we did them
> fragile as cabbage moths
> our white dresses flicking in sunlight[5]

A Day Dress

I married a man who wrote a thesis about what happens to the plots of nineteenth-century novels when the heroine inherits property. It seemed about books then and yet now it seems close to life as well, to Mary's life and her matrilineal legacy. I can imagine the unfinished purple silk garment would be most suitable as a day dress for a Dorothea or a Little Dorrit or indeed just our Mary. Mary in transit from Ireland to New Zealand, from Victoria to Perth, or just across the road from *Cathay* to the sofa. Mary with her tiny waist and her curls and her Irish chin; who, when she hugged you, bristled with dressmaker's pins.

Casa Materna: A Coda

... is the mother house with the ghostliest coordinates in my family tree. I can't begin to tell its story here because that would be to deviate from Mary's line. It is the name of a large house by the sea at Portici and concerns my sister, another Mary ... Maria, who was sent to this American-funded orphanage as a girl. It is a story, not unlike a nineteenth-century novel, about a family trying to stay together. And it concerns a seamstress too.

Years later, years since Mary, years since the orphanage, Maria and I are finally together. We're together in the house that is awash with cloth, sorting this and sorting that. We have projects and energies that seem to come from somewhere beyond the present. Windows are redressed, cushions recovered, clothes mended. We trawl through Mary's great cloth estate. *What is this, honey? And what is this?*

Even so, even then, the unfinished purple silk garment eludes me. I've learnt to love the potential granted from its unlocatable, partially made state. Things are nothing. They lie doggo, they can tell us something about the people in proximity to them but not everything. Some things persist but they are just little scraps and hints.

*

Purple is also the colour of some wild thing overlooked, *a violet by a mossy stone,* the skin beneath my second child's eyes, the insides of cockleshells, and the jacaranda bells falling and falling. The slide to summer – *l'estate.*

With thanks to Lesley Dougan, Josephine Wilson, and Tony Hughes-d'Aeth.

The Trouble with Purple – Annamaria Weldon

The ship was suddenly there: 2,700 years since it sailed, thirty years after I had left the Mediterranean to live on the other side of the world in Western Australia, and just as I was drafting this essay. The image glowed from my iPhone screen. A Phoenician trading vessel surrounded by turquoise water off the coast of Gozo, my grandfather's native island, in the Maltese archipelago. My inner poet wants to write that it floated on my Facebook news-stream, but floating was not what it was doing.

The pictures were submarine, for I was looking at freshly discovered wreckage in pristine condition. The discovery and its location had been kept secret for the past month, during which the find was added to the Inventory of Cultural Treasures of Malta. When announced, it made world headlines. Three countries became engaged in the recovery effort and ensuing research. Because Malta was a significant dot on the historic purple trade route, about which so little is known, expectations are high that this ancient vessel and its cargo will prove to be a kind of Rosetta Stone.

I was born in my maternal grandpa's home on the main island, which was so central to the Phoenicians' seafaring trade in purple dye. When he was a young man, my paternal grandfather had crossed the channel from Gozo to live in Malta while he attended university. He was the first of his family to do so, eventually became Chief Justice of Malta and was knighted by the late King of England. But to us he was just Nannu Turo, who remained proudly 'Gozitan'.

Gozo, overlooked by the chain of colonisers who conquered Malta, had retained its traditional agrarian and fishing culture. This hilly little island produces an abundance of fruit and vegetables and its bread is the best I have ever tasted. As our family's second home, its history was ours: my parents honeymooned there during World War II, and my London-based brother, now in his sixties, still holidays on the island every year. When we were children, each June at the start of the summer holidays, Nannu Turo and my grandmother Nanna Nusa returned to their tiny Gozitan beachfront home at Marsalforn Bay. The flock of cousins which followed them across the channel for this annual migration included us.

On the island we spent all the hours of daylight outdoors, in the sea, by the sea or on it in small boats. After dark, youngsters were allowed to roam the fishing village, where all the families knew each other. We congregated along the sea wall, or in side streets wherever anyone was playing a guitar on their doorstep. We made sorties to the only shop (no bigger than a bathroom), which sold ice-creams and fizzy drinks. The adults were at café tables playing cards, or strolling along the seafront, stopping from house to house to greet friends resting on wicker chairs or the low walls of the small tiled area outside each front door, called the 'parapet'. It was too hot to stay indoors in the late 50s and early 60s, as there was no air conditioning or even fans in remote, rural Marsalforn. I remember oil lamps, my grandmother's lighting ritual each evening: that dramatic flare of bright and shadow they threw on the uneven surface of interior stone walls, and bedtime's acrid smell of extinguished wicks.

I had never before been part of such a great amorphous crowd of relatives and friends. After spending a decade overseas, mostly in London, my family had just returned to live in Malta on the cusp of my teen years. Those first summers – when I was an outrider fish, skirting the school of youngsters as it darted and dived through the dark streets – felt like the beginnings of belonging. As the only daughter of strict parents I was unaccustomed to the social freedom that blessed our summers in Gozo, where I was part of the large sub-group collectively known as 'the Mercieca cousins', some who had their own family summer houses in the bay, others like us who always headed to Nannu's home for meals and to sleep. There were often times when eight of us shared the room which served as a dormitory in the two-up, two-down sandstone terraced house. I remember lying in bed late at night as we whispered in the dark, while moonlight reflected on the shiny beach pebbles we had set out on the windowsill – and I remember the embarrassment of having to use the toilet, where the ancient chain-pull made such a crashing sound. I remember the fascination as I watched the gutting of fresh fish caught by neighbours, and my excitement as I waited for the chinking bells which heralded a small herd of goats arriving each afternoon to be milked into enamel jugs at our kitchen door.

Nannu had always seemed very old and venerable. When I was nineteen and he was in his late nineties, he became gravely ill and, typically, eschewed hospital care for the ministrations of his devoted wife, mother of their eight children. As summer came in that year and his illness progressed, he seemed to live merely on the salted breath of his beloved Marsalforn Bay, so his bed was placed across the open balcony door, where he could feel its every caress and see the Mediterranean if he opened his eyes. When he closed them for the last time, the island's two main (and fiercely rival) band clubs argued over who would do the funeral honours and escort his cortege to the ferry, for burial on the main island. Eventually they settled on a very Gozitan solution: Nannu's hearse would be driven up the hill from his home to the capital Rabat, not once but *twice,* giving each band club a turn at leading his farewell procession.

*

The discovery of a Phoenician wreck in those shallow Gozitan waters was announced on the international news just ten days after I had shared these memories in the multicultural session of last year's Perth Poetry Festival, together with poems I had recently written about Gozo's coastal place names, and photos to illustrate them. Images of the buttery sandstone fortress walls round Rabat's ancient fortress capital Medina, on the island's highest hill; the turquoise bay waters; cerise and purple wildflowers growing in the shallow soil deposits of the island's craggy *garigue*. The timing of this marine discovery seemed doubly synchronous. I had just begun to write about my 'ancestral' connection to purple, so my first thought and question was: how long will it take for investigators to discover which amphorae had contained purple dye? Survey photos of the wreck, where it lay 130 metres deep, showed fifty amphorae still intact and scattered in the surrounding sand. These containers were of diverse shapes, each a distinct signature indicating that the ship had visited many different harbours and was indeed a trading vessel.

My imagination soared beyond this essay as I pictured possibilities for a book-length poetry project. I already had plans underway to visit Gozo in the new year after an absence of almost a decade, following an invitation to deliver a paper at the University of Malta. Perhaps that would provide me with an opportunity to meet some of the Phoenician wreck research team … Before long I was daydreaming about an island writing residency.

And then I remembered that a clairvoyant had once offered me a swatch of coloured cards, or fabric (the details are fuzzy) and I picked purple, which is when she told me, *That colour will bring you nothing but trouble.* The prediction seemed overly dramatic. But it did suggest an image to me, a coloured thread running through the tapestry of my life, only occasionally visible on the topside of the fabric. Could I, should I, avoid purple in the future? As the White Queen remarked to Alice, *It's a poor sort of memory that only works backwards.*[1]

Early in adolescence I had learned of the link between my Maltese heritage and the Phoenician trade in purple dye. I promptly adopted the colour. The phase survived unkind remarks (a schoolfriend's observation that I was *possessed by purple* and the summer party where my aunt's friend said to me, too loudly: *Few people can wear that colour, Anna, and you are not one of them*). I wonder, now, whether purple became my opium for the pain of non-entity? The experience of returning to my birth island after a nomadic childhood in Africa, the UK and Central America had equipped me with exotic memories in which nobody was interested, and left me totally ignorant of face-saving local knowledge. A foreigner in my own culture, ignorant of the vital sequence of feast days with their associated foods and customs which shaped island life, illiterate in Maltese, the local language which still permeated everyday discourse, although 'out of fashion' in colonial Malta where fluent English speakers were privileged (my one advantage), I muddled the names of my sixty-four first cousins and the twenty aunts and uncles to whom I had been so suddenly introduced and who were now central to our family's social life. What meagre sense of belonging I had mustered came from religion.

Being a Roman Catholic was a kind of citizenship: no matter where we lived, my family were devout churchgoers and I was educated by nuns. In those days of a universal Latin liturgy, the sense of shared sacred history and symbolism was as powerful as a tribal sense of place. It gave me known terrain, enriched by poetry remembered by heart; its seasons were easily distinguished by their prayers, music or ritual colours; its archetypal characters and stories patterned my imagination. The most transformative times in the church calendar, the traditional observances which reinforced our identity as Catholics were Lent and Easter, Advent and Christmas. These were magical and emotional events. Passages of transition and waiting, dread and longing. They were always celebrated in purple, that colour between hope and uncertainty.

Silken purple. Brocaded purple. Opulent purple. Priests robed in purple vestments, the interior walls of high cathedral and village church alike entirely hung with purple cloth. Tabernacles sheathed in purple. Still significant to this day, it is a colour code from ancient times, when cathedral stained-glass windows were storybooks for the illiterate, and a change of vestments signalled the beginning and end of sacred seasons.

To the devout, the long weeks of Lent and Advent exist in 'time out of time'. They are not, in liturgical parlance, 'ordinary time'. And although, in this post-Christian era, Lent and Advent are invisible to the secular world, back then I was not in the secular world most of the time. Throughout high school I spent the scholastic year in a convent. Obliged to wear what I thought was a particularly ghastly winter uniform and assigned a cubicle barely big enough for my bed, chair and washstand, I compensated with purple striped sheets, a purple bedcover and purple plastic water-jug and bowl. This gesture of individualism was a whim my mother indulged. She had no say in where I was schooled but she understood my resistance to conformity, detested convents and loved colour. As it turned out, the convent shaped me for life and also, I think, for the better. I made lifelong friendships, fell in love with literature and learned to live with less. But that realisation only came with hindsight.

*

There are many such paradoxical turning points in anyone's life. Mine have a colour signature. Was it prescience or protest when in my late forties I chose to wear a pale purple cape and carry purple liliums at my second wedding? Through divorce and remarriage, I broke faith with the rules of Catholicism. My soulmate was Wayne, a retired career soldier and wounded survivor of the Vietnam War. So in the Anglican co-cathedral that day I also carried red poppies and rosemary for remembrance, with golden ears of wheat for rebirth. And following Wayne's unforseen death just nine months later, I wore that shade of pale purple again, obsessively.

*

But that was eighteen years ago. Today, I've been reading outside, shaded by the Chinese elm. If there were grass in my Australian garden and were I younger, I would read spread-eagled on the earth, just the way I did in the Maltese convent grounds during the sacred retreats of Lent and Advent, when classes were suspended, time slowed and my friends and I spent our free time outdoors, reading. So long as we kept the ritual silence, the convent grounds were ours to roam – even the nuns' cemetery where plain gravestones impressed us with the visible permanence of lifelong enclosure.

The living community, with its school, dormitories and chapel, was housed in an old two-storey limestone building, its centre wrapped around a quadrangle. Like a chateau, it dominated the crest of St Julian's hill, surrounded by terraced fields, trees and garden walks with views of the Mediterranean below. Perhaps these contemplative interludes were an attempt to recruit us to Holy Orders, though none of us joined up. But they were also a gift. Reverend Mother's library books, which we could only borrow on feast days and retreats, immersed us in the improbable dramas of *The Lives of Saints*; assisted by frequent singing of hymns and the intoxicating smell of freesias, narcissus and stock growing all around us, we journeyed to the inner world. Decades later when I read of Pluto and Persephone, the young girl he took from Demeter as she lay on a hillside dazed by the smell of narcissus, I thought of our retreats.

Across the quad, inside the shadowy chapel, an open door by St Joseph's side-altar framed sunlit fields and you could hear the distant, rhythmic song of hoeing and cicadas. That cool interior smelt of candlewax, incense and wood-polish. In spring and autumn the whitewashed walls and white marble sanctuary were hung with glowing silk brocades of liturgical purple. The rich cloth also draped the altar, curtained the tabernacle, dressed the vestry side-walls and robed the visiting priest in drama. From childhood it had been the colour of non-ordinary time, ineluctably associated with the weeks leading to Christmas, or Lent's anticipatory grief. In my adolescence, during those days of silence and reflection, that purple's fatal beauty heralded encounters with the sublime.

*

Ever since the image of that ancient shipwreck appeared on my Facebook newsfeed, the possibility of composing a book-length suite of poems narrating Malta's place on the purple trade route has tantalised me. But because my writing process requires total immersion, researching that project would demand time and travel. From 2009 to 2014, writing *The Lake's Apprentice*, I was spellbound by the natural history of Yalgorup's wetlands, its communities, cultural stories and creatures. That would happen again if I took the Mediterranean as a location – and I'm not sure if it is how or where I want to spend the next five years. On the other hand, returning to my birth island, to its landscape and language, for an extended stay would reunite me with friends, family and island culture, which might prove the perfect opportunity for new writing. So I've vacillated, attracted by the creative possibilities but reluctant to commit to the challenges of such a project.

Which is why, halfway through writing this essay, while researching the Phoenician trade routes, I came across the Genographic Project[2] and resolved to let science decide my direction. When some of the Maltese male population had been tested, DNA indicating direct Phoenician ancestry was found in such a high percentage of samples that it led geneticist Pierre Zalloua of the American University of Beirut to speculate, 'Perhaps when the Phoenicians settled, they killed off the existing population, and their own descendants became today's Maltese.'[3] Surely, I thought, it would be a strong prompt to follow the story back, through time and through poetry, if I were to find out my family was part of that group.

The DNA testing kit soon arrived by post. It was simple to

use: two swabs were provided with which to take a sweep of each cheek from inside my mouth, and then I sealed them in little glass vials provided and popped them inside a padded, pre-addressed envelope which also came with the kit. As I handed over my completed 'parcel contents declaration', the post office assistant remarked it would take eight to ten days for the package to reach Texas. I walked back to the car calculating when I could expect the results, which according to the information pack would be available online within six to eight weeks of my test swabs reaching the lab.

Temporarily freed from worrying about the future, I delved into the past and found the story of purple full of portals to poetry. There are as many nuances to the mysteries of the dye's origins as there are shades of its colour. Making purple dye was historically a great deal of trouble, not least for the muricid sea snails from which the chemical precursor of the requisite dye compound was harvested. In a harrowing process, the mollusc's hypobranchial gland was exposed by cracking and peeling off the back of its shell (I have found no evidence to reassure me the unfortunate molluscs were killed prior to this process). The viscous fluid was then extracted by hand using a sharp tool to scrape out the glandular secretions. It is at this point, as cells begin to die, that a chemical process is initiated which most probably led to the discovery of that precious, colourfast purple dye. The process continues with complex chemical interactions associated with decomposition, oxidisation and debromidisation by means of light, all of which have to be carefully monitored and controlled, adding to the expense of collection and production. As the writer Vitruvius succinctly documented in the first century BCE, 'Purple exceeds all colors in costliness and superiority of its delightful effect. It is obtained from a marine shellfish ... It has not the same shade in all the places where it is found, but is naturally qualified by the course of the sun.'[4]

Although still referred to as *Murex*, the genus of sea snail defined originally by Linnaeus, the current name for the marine gastropod mollusc to which Vitruvius probably referred is *Hexaplex trunculus* (the banded dye-murex), which is native to the Mediterranean. However, though this was possibly the Phoenicians' mollusc of choice, it is not the only one useful in creating purple dye nor was the manufacture of purple dye confined to the Mediterranean. The most cursory online research reveals associations with woad and whelks in Britain, labour-intensive traditional dye practices still practised in Mexico involving local shellfish, traces of purple dye in ancient parchment, illustrated manuscripts, archaeological finds from as far east as Japan, murals and burial cloths. In a further tantalising twist, there is evidence from ancient breeding tanks that these molluscs, which are carnivorous, displayed cannibalistic behaviour when stressed by the conditions of their confinement.

As a nature writer whose inspiration is most often found at the interstice of biology and art, I find these details irresistible. I began to be glad that my DNA test would not be conclusive, because as a woman, I don't have the Y chromosome which gives access to my father's deep ancestry; my sample indicates the maternal line and that is predominantly what would be explored in tracing my geographic roots. I knew my mother (who was a blue-eyed blonde) had family roots in Northern Italy, so when my result showed no Phoenician indicators in our lineage, I was already a step ahead, preparing to ask my brother to take the test. Michael lives in London, so I waited for one of our phone calls to explain my request. His willingness to help me discover whether there's a link on my father's side of the family delighted me, and in my excitement I began to describe how the fewer mutations on any type of DNA, the older it is deemed to be and the J2 Haplogroup, which indicates Phoenician descent, is estimated to be between seven thousand and twelve thousand years old.

Which is when he stopped me and said, 'Whoa! Just send me the link.'

'Thanks so much, Michael, the process won't cause you any problems,' I promised him, confident the clairvoyant was only talking about me when she predicted the trouble with purple. And what writer would want to avoid that?

The Red and the Blue: Confessions of an (Unlikely) Dockers Fan – Deborah Hunn

It's early on Saturday afternoon, September 21st, 2013, and I'm heading to the AFL Preliminary Final, Fremantle Dockers v Sydney Swans, at Pattersons Stadium in Subiaco. This is it. The penultimate hurdle to glory. 'At last,' I sing, channelling the tune, but not the talent, of the late Etta James. 'Freo, way to go', I sing, embracing the dagginess of our much (perhaps not unjustly) maligned club song. We've cleaned up at 'The Cattery' two weeks before, beaten the Geelong Cats down at Kardinia Park in the second qualifying final. In the process we've thrown the lyrics of their silly club song back in their faces, triumphing in a close, thrilling match against the odds of a typically sneaky Victorian fix that saw us piling additional travel time onto our Melbourne schedule by playing, not as tradition would have it, at the MCG or Docklands, but at the Cats' notoriously tricky home venue. We've proven to our coach Ross 'Rossy' Lyon that we can live up to our new mantra, 'anywhere, anytime';[1] our valour has earned us a break week, we're rested and reinvigorated and we know we can take the reigning premiers. We're on top of our game, the Swans are clearly hampered by injuries and attitude; we have the advantage of playing at home, with all the power and passion of the purple army – our own crowd of supporters – to drive us forward. Decked out in the team's hallmark purple colour, with our boys in their purple kit – purple jersey, three white chevrons, plus purple shorts with trademark anchor at the pleat – we'll send the Swans flapping back east to their harbour through the force of our famous purple haze.

*

'We, we, we ...' Since when have I readily embraced a 'we'? And with a sporting team? Why do the boys in purple inspire in me the willingness to deploy the plural pronoun and the pledge to the tribe that implicitly goes with it? Footy lovers get it of course, but friends (almost invariably female) who are not footy inclined look at best amused, at worst askance, as I enthuse both in person and on social media about my purple passion, readily employing the plural along the way. Yes, that's me. Uploading a muscled-up, fist-clenching Pav (team captain and club legend Matthew Pavlich for the uninitiated) as my profile photo on Facebook; posting pics of my newly acquired cat Purrseus proudly wearing his purple collar and sprawled out on the sofa, bedecked from ear to tail in my Dockers scarf; me sharing updates from various news and Dockers websites about our team's preparations; me uploading snaps I've taken on my phone of the profusion of purple that has started to flood Perth and Freo in the Finals weeks. Me, an academic with a PhD in literary and cultural studies, a writer and a teacher of professional and creative writing, a woman, a feminist, a queer? Me, the sceptic, me, who's not a 'team player'!

What's the deal, Deb? It's such a bloke's game. Full of macho boofheads – both on-field and off – sleazy sex scandals, overpaid boys behaving badly, drunken end-of-year shenanigans, lads around the barbecue in daft beer ads, drug cheats and punch-ups and foul-mouthed sledging of the 'I fucked your mother/sister/girlfriend' variety, not to mention the puerile, misogynistic antics of John 'Sammy' Newman, et al., on Channel 9's *The Footy Show*. Why?

The truth is, sometimes my purple passion puzzles me.

Maybe it's just a case of some girls do, some girls don't. Take my friends Colleen and Caroline: Caroline, a keen athlete, all-round sport lover and Dockers fan comes along with me to the Dockers–Sydney preliminary final. She responded with unabashed glee when I told her I could get my hands on tickets; Colleen, definitely not footy oriented, a passionate art lover but not much of a sports fan, surprised us suddenly, saying she'd like a ticket also, to show willing, to see what all the fuss was about. Then she found out the price. Expletive deleted! And even though Caroline offered to pay her way, the price was not worth what she was sure would be the boredom of the event. Indeed, why would money be spent on such a thing, when it could go instead on the pursuit of aesthetic fulfilment? She'd rather visit an art gallery, or go shopping – and she did, later taking great pleasure in pointing out that she'd bought a couple of pairs of beautifully handcrafted Spanish espadrilles online for the same price.

I, however, wouldn't have surrendered my ticket for a truckload of fascinating footwear, and while I'm not much of a shopper at the best of times I'm hardly a complete freak among females for putting a footy final first. For all the blokeyness of the culture, Aussie Rules, like all the big, male-dominated sporting codes, has traditionally had female fans aplenty, and they can be found in all ages, races, sexual preferences, occupations and ethnicities. You just have to go to a game, or more telling still perhaps, watch one on TV as the cameras pan the crowd in response to a controversial umpiring decision to see, framed in close-up, gesticulating girls and growling grannies alike directing well-seasoned advice to the 'white maggots' (these days dressed in almost anything but white) on such subjects as where they can stick their umpire's whistle.

In fact, over the last decade or so the AFL and its clubs have sought to address the gender divide and the kind of sexism that, as Miriam Cannell's 1997 documentary *Game Girls* amply testifies, ritually beset female sports commentators like the pioneering Caroline Wilson. Most notably, according to the AFL Community website, the 2005's AFL Respect and Responsibility Policy works to ensure that 'people throughout the AFL are aware and have structures in place that recognise that violence against women and behaviour that harms and degrades women, is never acceptable.'[2] Initiatives which work to support the officially stated key principles of 'respect', 'responsibility' *and* 'participation' range from academic consultants and education workshops for male players, to increased participation by women in AFL administration and board memberships, to women runners and goal umpires (well there seem to be one or two who feature fairly regularly), to little girls getting a guernsey along with their boy cohorts in half-time Auskick, to support for female players through development, sponsorship and provision of information about competitions and achievements. When I scroll across the AFL Community website section dedicated to 'Female Football'[3] it certainly seems a long way from the days of several decades ago, when this little barefoot tyke sped around the backyard pretending to be one of her WAFL heroes – usually the diminutive quick-as-a-flash East Fremantle goal sneak, Tony 'Budgie' Buhagiar – all the while grumbling that only boring bloody netball and hockey were on offer as winter sports for girls.

This said, the brave new world of sensitive new-age footy is not quite as reconstructed as it appears. The reality is that women who play the game still remain firmly on the outer paddock, devoid of the pay cheque and public recognition afforded to their male counterparts, while, as argued by Anna Krien in her powerful 2010 study, *Night Games: Sex, Power and Sport*,[4] despite the R&R code, double standards are still evident and young women who socialise off-field with players can find themselves negotiating behaviours ranging from casual misogyny and objectification to sexual abuse and a band of brothers/big-business network that seemingly closes ranks to protect its own. As for gay men, while the powers-that-be have, in fairness, certainly shown some recent efforts to be supportive, we have yet to see any AFL players 'come out', and meanwhile verbal slips by various football 'identities' make it pretty clear a culture of casual homophobia remains, despite whatever official or unofficial censures are brought to bear. Like many a Dockers supporter pursuing the everyday world of fandom, I've heard (or read on discussion boards) the alliterative and associative purple poofs and pansies thrown casually into the mix – or implied in the subtext – along with the perennial Shockers or sinking-anchors taunts; schoolyard stuff that's no less indicative of a homophobic mindset for being framed, as it sometimes is, as knowingly ironic or harmless jest, and undoubtedly a lot cruder when mobilised in the actual schoolyard.

Docker, femmo, lezzie, queer. Only the innocent or the irredeemably cynical can believe that colours are just decorative whims or markers to flog brands – they can show our loyalties, point to our passions and our vulnerabilities, shape and mark our identities, signify subversively, and sometimes, without intention, result in very strange bedfellows, in improbable points of unity. That's the case for me with purple and the various shades along its spectrum: Purple for the Dockers; the violet/purple in the Rainbow flag; purple, mauve and lavender with their network of historical associations with queerness, from Oscar Wilde to The Lavender Menace; the purple worn on days like IDAHO, May 17th, international day of action against homophobia, or Wear it Purple Day, in solidarity with bullied LGBT youth; even the purple of the suffragettes factors into the equation.

You've come a long way, baby. Well, one thing is for certain, in the fan stakes women are now a key market demographic courted by the AFL and its clubs, and are wooed with tempters designed to cater to what are perceived to be their tastes. For instance, as an $85 'add on' to my membership in the 'Purple Army', I have the option to join the official women's supporter group 'The Sirens', and thus '[e]njoy exclusive merchandise' (travel pillow, magnet photo frame, etc.) 'and events in the company of like minded ladies and build life-long friendships.'[5] I, however, am not a member of the Sirens. Needless to say, I can't quite envisage myself as one of Homer's temptresses, although in fairness the name seems an innocent attempt to draw on the club's brand-specific nautical theme, while also referencing a football term. Certainly, I struggle to see myself in the description of 'like minded lady', and just maybe I suspect, like Krien, that such gambits are less about equity and inclusion than they are about harnessing a hitherto undervalued resource. Mum's attendance, or her compliance with Dad's disappearing to the footy solo cannot be taken for granted anymore, nor can her willingness to let her boys play nasty brutish Aussie Rules, when seemingly softer sports like soccer beckon.[6] I should add though that I'm not such a sceptic as to knock the idea of women building life-long friendships, or to ignore the valuable outcomes of the work the club does in supporting charities and community initiatives. Indeed, I'm quietly proud of the fact – well, some may say it's more of a serviceable myth – that, with its strong immersion in the traditionally working-class and multicultural Fremantle community, its history of hard knocks and mishaps, a battler fan base and notable Indigenous player representation, the Dockers have an egalitarian appeal that – as the late Matt Price cheekily noted in his book about the trials and tribulations of Dockers fandom, *Way To Go*[7] – seems to stand in strong contrast to the blue-chip, establishment veneer of much vaunted cross-town rivals, the West Coast Eagles. This said, though, I can't quite exempt my team from Krien's shrewd feminist question about the AFL's public celebrations of 'forgotten heroes' and 'good women'. Yes, there is certainly evidence in the footy narrative of less traditional roles, new modes of participation, but it's hard to deny that the dominant representations in media and marketing remain: selfless mothers, nurturing support staff and, of course, glamorous WAGs on the red carpet. 'Are we changing stereotypes here,' Krien asks 'or simply reinforcing them?'[8]

It is a mode of representation that might, at a glance, seem exemplified by a recent article by Rosie Duffy on the Dockers website celebrating the one hundredth birthday of Margaret Doig, the devoted, unfailingly supportive 'matriarch of a famous

Fremantle football family' whose men played for WAFL clubs East Fremantle and South Fremantle for generations and who give their name to the Dockers annual award for best and fairest player, the Doig Medal: 'In 1937,' writes Duffy, 'she married East Fremantle football legend George Doig.' According to Margaret's eldest son Don, 'George and his brother Charlie played against Swan Districts the same day. After the match, they changed and walked across to the church, which is just across the road from the oval, to get to the altar on time.' Asked, some seventy-seven years after becoming a football bride, who her favourite Fremantle Dockers player is, she is lauded for a motherly diplomacy that handily endorses both continuance and community – 'I just love them all because they are Fremantle.'[9]

Mama Mia! And yet, while I understand (and share) Krien's concern with the persistence of stereotyping, when I look at the picture of stalwart, sweet-faced Mrs Doig, it's not just that I'm enough of a Dockers tragic to be charmed; more importantly I can't help but respect the hard yards, the years of emotional and physical labour that she has obviously put in – as indeed have so many women in the history of the game. It is not that this legacy of women's work (in the past, often taken for granted and obscured) should not be celebrated; rather, what matters is that this is not mobilised in such a way as to obscure a clear view of other stories, of problems that persist, and of empowering new possibilities of difference.

At a personal level, but one that I think crucially affects the way I, as a woman, relate to the game, the story also makes me think about my dad, an East Fremantle supporter from boyhood despite a western suburbs upbringing and stints at Melbourne Grammar and Guildford Grammar. He would have been fifteen in 1937, was devoted to the gritty, stylish East Freo, and worshipped greats like the Doigs. It was my father who indoctrinated not just his son, but his daughters – my sister and I – into his footy passion, regularly taking us all to games, telling us of the mighty team triumphs – not least of which was the great year of 1946, when the team won every single game they played. His stories filled me with the belief that the blue-and-white kitted Old Easts (this was before they took on the nickname The Sharks in the early 80s) with more premierships under their belt than any other WAFL team, could, perhaps in conjunction with erstwhile port town rivals – the tough, red-and-white kitted South Fremantle – one day produce a reunited Fremantle team (reunited, as there had once been a Fremantle team in the late nineteenth century). This dream team could enter a national competition and there prove mighty enough to topple the great Victorian teams of the evil VFL.

A few decades later – my father has passed away, I have returned from many years living interstate, and the once and future Fremantle team has duly emerged into the AFL and is rapidly proving itself, through a series of erratically played losing encounters, to be far from Arthurian. A young man in one of my tutorials tells me that the Dockers chose purple as one of the team colours because it was what you get when you mix blue and red: the two Freo teams, long locked in ferocious port-side rivalry ritually slugged out in twice-yearly derbies now, or so it would seem, improbably merged as one. Of course, experts would quickly note that the Fremantle Football Club did not have its roots as an AFL club in an actual merger of the existent East/South WAFL clubs. Moreover, I've never found any empirical evidence to support the tale of red+blue = purple. Official club historian Les Everett points to an initial marketing preference for purple as a unique and strong colour,[10] and his illustrated history of the club, along with G. A. Haimes' doctoral thesis on the club's organisational culture, indicate that purple is a colour known to have various traditional uses on the docks,[11] thus chiming in with the maritime associations of the other two colours that made up the original Dockers strip – red and green – which signify port and starboard respectively.

All very sensible no doubt, but for symbolism and sentiment, I still choose to believe in the mythic equation blue+red = purple.

By rights such romanticism, and such a heritage, should put me at the ground and out front of the purple cheer squad, week after week, but I tend to prefer watching the game in the privacy of my own lounge room, especially if there's a chance of rain. There, whether alone or in company, I can be found firmly planted in front of the TV for every Dockers game, exhibiting the full gamut of fanesque emotions: wearing my Dockers scarf, marvelling at the arcane knowledge, anecdotal detours and verbal eccentricities of the commentators, whistling and clapping when the boys run out, leaping off the sofa, fists clenched in evangelical triumph when a freakish Ballantyne or 'Son Son' Walters snap flies us to unlikely victory, marvelling at Mick Barlow's dogged determination in working a ball out of a tight pack, heart soaring as Nat Fyfe's haystack hair flies into the stratosphere, sighing at the graceful, laconic kicking style of defender Michael Johnson, puzzling at the perversely fierce defence of well known Baha'i follower Luke McPharlin, slumping head in hands in 'oh not again!' despair when a poster by Pav plummets us into yet another cycle of hell, celebrating with the club song when one of his monster kicks sails through and we rise again to fight another day.

Very occasionally I go to the game when a friend has a spare ticket, but I've been known to baulk if the seats aren't under cover and there's a chance of getting wet. Maybe there's a part of me rebelling against a childhood structured around Dad's regime of family footy visits, my little legs (I was the baby) sometimes struggling to keep up as we raced on a day of blustery winter weather from some far-away parking spot to make it for the first bounce. Maybe the sullen lefty-femmo arts student rejecting family tradition (including footy) still exerts her will occasionally, or maybe I just find (or so I like to kid myself) that the mediated spectacle on the TV screen provides superior coverage for the connoisseur, with its careful close-ups, multiplicity of angles and slo-mo replays. Then again, maybe I'm just lazy – my heart beats purple, but my guts are yellow and my failure to commit is down to dilettantism. Truth is, I fear at times that I'm a bit of a Clayton's supporter; Dockers-lite, not a battle-scarred true believer, ready to stand by my team come hell or high water.

On Saturday September 21st, 2013 though, I find myself humming with anticipation, filled with a sweet, uncomplicated buzz that takes me back to sunny childhood days of East Freo triumphs, and bounces me forward on the balls of my adult feet across Hadyn Bunton Avenue to meet Caroline at an appointed spot outside Gate 24. Around me the building crowd is a carnivalesque swirl of purple, tempered with the white trim, with chevrons and anchors and thick, bold FREO and DOCKERS lettering, flecked here and there with occasional hints of red and green, tangible reminders of the club's original red, green and purple strip, officially abandoned in 2010 for the superior recognition and marketing value of pure purple. The faithful are swaddled in scarves, caps, beanies, jumpers, hoodies, shirts and jackets; kids and adults shoulder Dockers bags and flags, carry banners, swish streamers and balloons. White inflatable anchors bob around, faces are painted purple and white, and someone hands me an A3 size poster, a wobbleboard to wave and shake our boys to victory. It's purple of course, with GO FREO in white block letters on one side and includes a triptych of heroes on the other: Danyle Pearce, Stephen Hill and Michael 'Sonny' Walters, all key team members and part of the Dockers' great tradition of fostering Indigenous talent – one of which I, like so many supporters, am genuinely proud.

I see a guy strolling past, fully rigged out in a snappy purple velvet suit – shades of 60s Carnaby St, barring the finishing touches of white trainers with purple stripes and a dark purple beanie. In my modest way I too wear my passion. I don't own a team jumper or jacket but I do have a non-merchandise purple polo of just the right shade which I wear over a black jumper. I have a Dockers cap too, a cheap knock-off, closer to maroon than purple, a joke gift from a tennis mate, a rusted-on Eagles fan, who won it in a Christmas work raffle and handballed it to me with pantomime disgust, on strict instructions that I never wear it against her on court. Local footy rivalry being what it is I've made sure to ignore her on key occasions, but for this serious footy outing the oddly maroonish colouring worries me and I shove it in my bag prior to reaching the ground. Getting your footy colours wrong is not an option, and heaven forbid anyone should mistake me for a displaced toothless Brisbane Lion! One sartorial touchstone is beyond doubt though: I have my Dockers scarf. It's an old and treasured item bought some years before from the store down at club headquarters at Fremantle Oval. And, because it predates the 2010 rebranding exercise, it's not just purple and white; it's red, green, white and purple.

I'm actually a fan of the new all-purple kit: after all, it's blue+red, it's distinctive, it's unique as a footy colour and, well, it's so wonderfully, unintentionally queer. But nevertheless, I have remained true to the old scarf because it seems to me (and comparing notes with others I know I'm not alone) that it signifies endurance. Call it overcompensation in my case at least, but this scarf says (to me at least) I'm no blow-in, I haven't just climbed on board because the team's started winning big, with a likely chance of a grand final. I've suffered, in my rather sheltered way, through near two decades long of winters of Dockers discontent that have now led to this glorious sun of September. The Shockers, the humiliating on-field cock-ups, false starts, the nearly made-its, the drubbing defeats, the endless ribbing from the commentators and the supporters of other clubs, especially Eagles fans, the next year in Melbourne predictions that fall flat, the brand new starts with another coach or a new repertoire of players, an important (albeit ageing) interstate star who turns out to be a dud, or else does stalwart but limited service before puttering out to grassture with a bung back or a dud hammy. I'm still here; we're still here – and now it's our turn.

Caroline and I touch base, both grinning, and begin the mountainous assent to our seats, scaling the stairs to the top tier of a big lump of ugly concrete behind the goals at the Subi end. It's normally the sort of windswept Stalinist tower I'd cite as evidence for the virtues of TV viewing, even though the big screens at either side of the ground these days provide more than adequate compensation. On this day though I'm as happy as Hillary, surveying the swarm of excited Dockers fans as they buzz in below and around me, interspersed by the blood-red of the Sydney Swans' faithful. I feel the concrete under my feet throb with the crowd's excitement. As we settle in, the boys are warming up, thumping practice shots into the temporary nets behind the goals, much to the thrill of kids pooling close by to watch. Then there's the hoopla of the pre-game entertainment, so banal I struggle to remember it, the bum-wiggling, foot-crunching manoeuvres as new arrivals in our row weave past, the juggling of beverages and the wafting aromas of richly fried and salted, onion-saturated and sauce drenched fast food, comparing notes with Caroline, killing time snapping photos on the mobile, the eruption of cheers and chants as the players finally run out and crash the banners, the due diligence to a national anthem that's about as daft as our club song (just who is this old duck Gert-by-sea?) the coin toss, the crowd exploding at the bounce ... our giant of a big man Aaron 'Sandy' Sandiland's fist crashing like Thor's hammer through the clouds ... *so this is why people GO to the footy!*

In the first quarter the game is as ugly as a street brawl. The Dockers mount a relentless forward press and lock down Sydney in a rolling maul of tackles; the pressure is blistering, but the kicking is wild, and by the siren we've managed a disappointing 2.9 to their 2.2. We should be streets ahead, but instead we're stuck revving at the intersection. The crowd vibe is still festive, but my gut tunes in to a collective twitching of nerves; an understandable reflex when you've spent twenty years watching your team invert the triumphal cliché – snatching defeat from the jaws of victory. Two old guys sitting next to us, with drawn, leathery faces beneath weather-worn Dockers caps, both with an ear dangling the small white cord of a transistor radio, exchange terse, worried words. I think of my dad, suspecting he'd tune a ready eye to these characters, and I imagine the impossible pleasure of having him beside me. Then I realise that 'the old guys' are probably closer in age to me at fifty-two than to him, at what would have been ninety-one. Time can be a relentless bastard of an opponent, and a trickster to boot, and in that moment I miss my father more intensely – and yet feel closer to him – than I have since his death.

Meanwhile, the game is on again and our boys – revved up by Ross Lyon – are flying goal-wards with a precision that now matches the intensity of their play. The crowd is ballistically pro-Docker, but just behind us a young guy in a Sydney jumper, chosen, so he informs the mates he's sitting with, not for affiliation, but with the express intention of pissing the purple people off, persists in niggling, offering spicy if increasingly redundant advice to Freo, until eventually one of the old guys tells him to 'watch his effing language'. The unfortunately contradictory choice of adjective brings guffaws from the recipient, but (and for all the daft, blokeyness of the exchange, I'm more than happy enough to own this) the last laugh is with us (me, the Dockers and the old guys) as a spectacular – and very accurate – second quarter closes with the purple firmly ahead 7.11 to 2.2. Now for a carton of those delicious salty, hot chips – crisp on the outside, and warm and juicy with potato squish on the inside after the crunch. Junk food never tasted so good.

The Dockers maintain their dominance for the rest of the match, although a Swans fightback and a slight easing of scoreboard pressure by our boys towards the end of the game unleashes an eleventh-hour quiver of worry, with the final margin closing to twenty-five points. In the last five minutes, though, it is clear we simply can't be beaten and the ground begins to echo with one short repeated riff. It's not the seesawing Freeee-ohh, Freee-ohh we've come to expect, but something cryptic that I find myself chanting like a mantra before I fully grasp its meaning: MCG,

MCG, MCG, MCG, and MCG. Yes, that's where we're going. Tomorrow in Jerusalem; next Saturday in Melbourne. We're off to challenge for the Holy Grail.

A week later, unable to make it away from Perth, I watch the game on TV with my mother at her nursing home, proud but ultimately gutted as, despite the gusto of the mighty purple army that floods over to Melbourne to cheer them on, the Dockers falter horribly at the MCG – a slow start, wasted opportunities in front of goal, and then a desperate, gutsy lunge to come back too late at the end. I speculate, like many a pundit, that maybe the big occasion overpowered the ingénues. I concede that maybe – just maybe – our wily and experienced opponents Hawthorn were just too good. I wax mythical too – we stumbled because we were forced to wear our away strip for the match: the white jumper adorned with purple chevrons and white shorts. Unfair advantage to the Vics of course! We're just like poor old Samson with his hair shorn. Mum listens to all this with a sympathetic, diplomatic nod and a cheeky, happy little glint in her eye. She's a Melbourne girl by birth and upbringing, and a football lover who accompanied us to all those East Fremantle games, gamely supporting her husband's team, then went over to the Eagles with the AFL entry in the late 80s and stayed there. Whenever the Eagles are out of the equation though, she gets a double dip, reverting to the Melbourne team of her youth – Hawthorn.

Normally that cheeky little glint would rile me – smug Victorians! Given her increasing frailty, the slow but relentless tax that a recent diagnosis of Alzheimer's has begun to impose upon her memory, I find myself – however frustrated by the Freo loss – checking my response, pulling back into perspective to cherish her enjoyment of the occasion and my luck to be sharing the experience of 'that one day in September' with my mother one more time. Later, when I start to write this essay, I will remember that purple is the chosen colour of the Alzheimer's Association.

Colours, as I observed earlier, are not just decorative whims or markers to flog brands: they can indeed show our loyalties, point to our passions and our vulnerabilities, shape and mark our identities, signify subversively, and sometimes, without intention, result in very strange bedfellows, in improbable points of unity. At the close of the preliminary final, as the chant 'MCG MCG MCG' continued to ring out amid the ecstatic celebrations after the siren, anything seemed possible. While many stayed behind, continuing their celebrations, Caroline and I began our descent down the grey concrete tower, a journey that allowed me to see through the back of each tier and into the bays just below. In the crisp cold air of early spring dusk, enhanced by the beams of the activated stadium lights, these bays full of faithful seemed bathed (blessed, dare I say it?) in a luminescent purple glow. The intensity of the colour was heightened, hypnotic – like the illumination of a stained-glass window by a gently setting sun. I felt infused – there is no other verb to describe it – with an odd blend of awe and serenity, with a sense of connection, an effortless melding into a communal spirit which I suddenly recognised as akin to the emotion I'd experienced as a participant in Pride parades, walking in solidarity with my tribe through Northbridge, amid the cheers, the glitter, the dazzle of the streetlights, the swirling rainbow colours.

Afterword

In early 2015, at the same time as this piece was being finalised for publication, the AFL announced that one NAB Challenge pre-season clash would be themed as an official Pride match. The teams involved would be the Sydney Swans and the Fremantle Dockers and the match, to be played in Sydney, would coincide with Sydney's Gay and Lesbian Mardi Gras. Mark Evans, the AFL football operations manager commented: 'Diversity and inclusion is essential to our game. We say, "no matter who you are, where you are from or who you love, we can all love footy".'[12] On March 15th, on an oval featuring distinctive rainbow markings, Sydney defeated Fremantle by nine points.[13] I have never been prouder of my team.

The Two Loves – Lily Chan

Life without Krishna has no joy for me. Tell me what is good for me. I am a wanderer with a hollow heart.
    Mahabharata, Book Sixteen: The Battle With Clubs

I fell in love with Krishna when I was three years old. I gazed at the wall fresco in Gopal's restaurant while my parents took turns feeding me sultana *halva* drowned in custard; I would point at the peacock feather tucked in his turban, the flute, the bangles circling his ankles. His skin was a deep blue, almost purple – his eyes luminous, pink palms turned upward.

Krishna was adopted and raised by a *gopi* in a rural village. He ran free in the forest with cowherds and goatkeepers, farmers and cows, indulging in pranks and stuffing clay and soil into his mouth. 'Come now, open up. What's in there,' the *gopi* said, tilting his head back and gazing in. In his mouth she saw the universe. The galaxies whirling at the base of his throat; the planets and stars and cosmic dust; even hundreds of reflections of her own self taking Krishna onto her lap. 'Millions of skies are within me,' he said.

My four siblings and I ran around barefoot on our farm in Narrogin. We scoffed at city cousins who winced at the hard gravel and red dirt, the ants and dry gumnut scrubble. Under the shed lived a menagerie of carpet snakes, blue-tongue lizards, drop-tail geckos, spiders and rats. Possums scrambled up trees and mated loudly on the roof. Magpies warbled greetings at dawn. We meditated and chanted sanskrit mantras on a thrice-daily regime, where family meals were vegetarian, egg-free, rennet-free, gelatin-free. We met the concept of indulgence, of material gluttony, with an austere shudder. We were nothing like Krishna. Krishna was perpetually flirtatious, bacchanalian in his appetites and as urgently boyish as Peter Pan; he broke into houses, gorged on curd pots and hid the clothing of *gopis* as they bathed. At a touch of his hand the rotting fruit became jewels, the hunchback woman straightened, the six dead children rose again, the magical flute played on and hypnotised all the listeners into a daze.

By the time I turned ten, I felt like a traitor for switching my affections from Krishna to Sai Baba. Sai Baba was the man of miracles from a small village in South India. It was said that he plucked all kinds of fruit from a wish-fulfilling tree, fruit out-of-season and grown in regions far away. I heard accounts of his materialisations, statues rising up from his palm, jewels and rings and pendants, of stone turning into candy, of how he appeared in two different places at once, rescuing followers from car accidents and train crashes and suicidal follies – how he suddenly turned up at the door of a professor in Osaka and hugged him, how he tore up visa applications and granted them for another in New Zealand – he was omnipresent and omniscient, he could travel at the speed of light, he knew everything.

The route from the Bangalore airport to the ashram in South India was well travelled by taxis and buses, wending through rural villages and outposts and boys hurrying cattle along with switches, the shrines built by the roadside adorned with desiccated petals and metal gods. Chalk mandalas dotted the ground. We waited in gender-segregated lines for *darshan*. He floated about the ashram grounds in a robe of saffron orange, a slight figure crowned in a dense black afro which seemed to wax with the moon, waving his hands in a circular motion and distributing ash to followers who daubed it between the eyes and swallowed clots of it as a reminder that all things are reduced to ash, all things are transient. His eyes were piercing yet gentle, his nose broad but somehow cute against his heavy cheeks.

The ashram was a global village of followers, a swelling ocean of people sprawled across the grounds and living in the pastel pink and white buildings which resembled, from a distance, thickly iced cakes. Garlands wrapped pillars. Volunteers swept the pathways and ushered tourists along. The washermen returned the laundry washed, dried and folded neatly in tone-matched piles. We attended a regimen of prayers, lectures and devotional singing. Sai Baba's lectures were translated and compiled into multiple anthologies. He insisted that the epics of the *Mahabharata* and the *Ramayana* had actually occurred; that Krishna once walked the earth; that fantastical giants and talking animals populated forests and cities; and at the utterance of a *mantra*, chariots would fly across the sky. My palms were inscribed in henna by an Indian woman who refused payment: 'It is a blessing for you, keep you safe.' I began wearing bangles and anklets, clapped harder during the *bhajans* in order to hear the instrumentals resonating from my wrist. In our spartan room in the residential towers, we crawled along to the spectre of diarrhoea and vomiting – sipping red cordial and ingesting charcoal tablets. The ceiling fan vibrated with the rhythm of *Vedic mantras*.

> Oṃ bhūr bhuvaḥ svaḥ
> tát savitúr váreṇyaṃ
> bhárgo devás yadhī mahi

> We meditate upon that most meditation-worthy
> the most knowable and hence
> the most relishable self-luminous radiance

In one of my dreams Krishna morphed into Sai Baba. Sai Baba's afro-haloed face hovered on Krishna's body as he played the flute and danced. 'You can call me Krishna Baba!'

I woke in euphoria – they were one and the same. Like nesting Russian babushka dolls, Krishna's lineage could be linked to Sai

Baba as *avatars* of the super god, Vishnu, he who floated through each of the ages of the earth and descended in embodied human form whenever righteousness and virtue were in decline – a kind of superman reincarnating himself over and over in different bodies.

Sai Baba never spoke to me in person. Yet I felt as if I owned him, I formed an intimacy, a projection mythologised by his followers. We exchanged stories of his divinity, how he had read our minds, hearts, directed our lives in such small and significant ways, passed around totems he had materialised, rings and necklaces, brooches and pictures. His grace was a vaccine, it was some kind of giant and invisible dome within which we were inoculated against the tribulations of the world. I tried my best to be worthy of his grace and resist the pull of pop culture and other things extraneous to the pursuit of spiritual enlightenment, but upon returning to Narrogin and entering high school I listened to Kyle and Jackie O on the radio – watched *Passions* and *The Bold and the Beautiful* when my parents were out – and browsed old copies of *Women's Weekly* and *Cleo* stashed in my wardrobe. For a Wheatbelt town over two hours drive from the nearest beach we were rather obsessed with surfing fashion. We wore Roxy boardshorts, Quiksilver thongs and appliquéd Billabong logos in purple glitter on our bags. Form class was an excuse to recap on *Home & Away* and *Neighbours*. The wooden desks were gouged by generations of students: affirmations of love, obscenities, clumps of dried gum, stickers from mandarins and Granny Smith apples. In the school canteen I gazed upon the crumbed and deep fried cornjack in awe. The farm kids stayed at the hostel or came in by the busload with the hardened skin of those used to rising at dawn and herding sheep and shooting them in times of drought, of downing beer before they reached fifteen and brushing their teeth in soda. Their pet lambs ended up in the fridge, heads crowning the kitchen bench in pools of coagulated blood. My classmates took orders for burgers, fries and milkshakes to the nearest Hungry Jacks on the outskirts of Perth, a four-hour return drive.

I nursed seasonal crushes on unattainable boys although our interactions did not progress much further than questions such as, 'Why did you end up in Narrogin – why did you move here?' A jolt ran through me when I confronted my Asiatic reflection in the mirror. I longed to be less apparent. During my first year of high school I plunged into a state of anxiety. I spent recess locked in a toilet stall or in the library corralled with books. The classes were bewildering and filled with teenagers engaged in quick and provocative conversations I could not follow. My tongue felt slow and my mind foggy. My thoughts turned with greater frequency towards Sai Baba. I wore his face in a small pendant around my neck and told onlookers he was my boyfriend. I scribbled requests onto notes and folded them inside the shrine enclosing his framed photo; prayers to vanish my acne and obtain my driver's licence, to pass my exams with marks above ninety. I gave him a pet name.

My meditations were adventures on a nightly trajectory, where I could sense the verge of the universe, the impression of limitless power, the globe circling beneath my fingertips, as if the secrets of life itself were about to be revealed. Purple was the colour of revelation – the moment just before the lotus opens in a light-filled meditation where we move the spore of light through every limb of the body and then expand it outwards until the universe is encompassed in light with such intensity that sweat ran down my face. In my last dream of Sai Baba I was sitting an exam with questions on my spiritual grade: *What are the attributes of god? What does god mean to you?* I flung down my pencil. I had passed the exam and yet there was no need to pass. Sai Baba walked past slowly in his orange robe and smiled at me. When the tertiary entrance exams were over I celebrated with my classmates. We slurped ice-cream spiders and shopped along Narrogin's main street – lavender-scented soaps, homewares, Target Country clothes. Our next destination was Perth, the city of traffic lights and palm trees, an adult city packed with unknown and dangerous things. I was terrified and excited. The horizons of my small, intricately constructed ashram were shifting.

More than a decade later and this all seems innocuous; these teenage attempts to pass various examinations of the spirit, to graduate from ignorant acolyte to illumined being, the continual self-progression and inquiry. These episodes of devotion and obsession appear dreamlike; it is as if I emerged from a haze. Yet I miss that utter immersion, that dome of invisible protection, and still the scent of turmeric and spice brings it back, as do glimpses of afro-haired pedestrians, Hare Krishna dancers in the street, the intricate stringed *veena* and the ululating sounds of devotional *bhajans*, the insignia of the OM curling in on itself in graffiti and tattoos – a hybridised India of Western appropriation and esotericism, a spiritual fusion, a global mishmash. The two loves are inseparable – Krishna fading into Sai Baba, Sai Baba's smile merging into Krishna's mysterious one, Krishna's inscrutable gaze matching Sai Baba's distant one, my longing for certainty.

Once I was an evangelist, a shy and secretive one holding the god inside a cheap locket, a necklace, a Post-It note prayer, a blu-tacked ring, and it seemed that the whole world would become unlocked and apparent to me in an instant of illumination, and the town where I lived would no longer be a mystery to me. I looked covertly for potential converts. The Golden Age of illumination could be a long time coming, but it would still come. Now I relish this new freedom. There is a vacancy of meaning. It is the mystery of the moment which keeps revealing itself without any reason or explanation, where karma holds no sway.

Glossary

avatar. Deliberate descent or incarnation of a holy deity on earth.
bhajan. Hindu devotional song.
darshan. In Sanskrit, auspicious sight or the beholding of a divine being.
gopi. In Sanskrit, a cow-girl.

halva. A sweet Indian dessert often made out of semolina.
Mahabharata and *Ramayana*. Two major and ancient epics from India, tracing the conflicts and dynasties of royalty and interactions with *avatars*.
mantra. Sacred utterance, numinous sound, or a group of syllables or words believed to have psychological and spiritual resonance.
Vedic. The language of the *Vedas*, being ancient and holy scriptures and verses composed in Sanskrit.
veena. Plucked stringed instrument with a bulbous end, originating in ancient India.

Purple Impressions – Rosemary Stevens

There was no blinding moment or first love with Impressionist art. Not that I recall, anyway. More a gentle osmosis: the Degas prints from childhood ballet days, the nude towelling her neck in my teenage bedroom, and the Renoir painting I now know as *Bal du Moulin de la Galette*. Its dappled warmth presided over every meal at the Rabauds', the couple I like to think of as my adopted French parents. Through a haze of wine at the weekend, our faces resonant with those of the Renoir, I could reimagine the flea-ridden gloom of my student flat in Bordeaux. Whenever I see that painting, conflated now in my mind with the Rabauds' hospitality, I bask in those effulgent blues and pastels, a twenty-year-old again.

The epiphany with Impressionism comes decades later, and it is through the colour purple in Melbourne. The sign on the wall reads: AUSTRALIAN IMPRESSIONISTS IN FRANCE, Ian Potter Centre, NGV: 15 June – 6 October 2013. Beneath it stands a woman about my own age, dapper in a black skirt and chartreuse blouse; nametag, Natasha. I saunter across, absorbing the quiet murmur of the anticipatory crowd. Then she gestures to us and we are led beyond the grey screen into a universe of colour.

The fierce tones of a Van Gogh assail us on the way in, with its crushed paper mountains and ectoplasm cloud. But Natasha sweeps on towards one of the main protagonists, *In the Morning, Alpes Maritimes from Antibes* (1890) by Australian Impressionist John Russell. We cluster around it, the rocky foreground and bleached coastal scrub suggesting an Australian scene, except for the pointillist lime in the foreground and the snow-capped mountains dreaming beyond a cool, green sea.

'Wow!' says the girl with the pink-tipped hair. 'All those lemony... limey tones...' the words slow to mirror our collective shift as we muse on the painting, '... and *purples!*'

Our mobiles are switched off, there are no clocks, no rush, no time; just this leisurely pace to match the heartbeat of the artist who captured this scene over a century ago. In a letter to Tom Roberts before beginning on the painting, Russell described the scene exactly as he saw it, in terms of colour: 'Sea a mighty blaze of blues, greens, purple, opalescent lights, distant snow covered Alps, tender green and rose sky. Over all a blaze of sunlight.'[1]

'Purple was much favoured by the Impressionists,' says Natasha, 'and for good reason.' And she tells us about the accidental discovery of this first synthetic dye by William Henry Perkin in 1856. The young chemist happened upon this brilliant hue, it appears, while trying to synthesise quinine for the treatment of malaria, and later commercialised it under the name 'Mauveine'. It was cheap to produce, colourfast and an instant hit, leading to the 'Mauve Decade' of the 1890s.

I glance around the gallery, and from every wall the colour throbs in violet cloud and scudding shade. Purple cliffs appear carved from colour; flesh takes on form, and under its spell, eyes acquire depth, and fabric substance. My lungs fill with a shock of recognition. Mauveine! That magical purple effect I've always felt from Impressionist art, but couldn't 'see' till now.

My mind flashes back to my seven-year-old self, falling under a different spell in the Birmingham Museum and Art Gallery; that of the Pre-Raphaelites whose purple melancholy and swoon-worthy scenes appealed to my English sensibilities. But Pre-Raphaelite purple is not at all mauveine; it's a sombre blend of madder root and cobalt blue, mixed on the pallet, according to tradition. Prior to this, purple was reserved to portray royalty, nobility and clergy, which is hardly surprising considering it took nine thousand snails to extract a single gram of pigment.[2] The Impressionists on the other hand broke with standard practice and applied their colours raw from the tube to be mixed in the eye of the beholder. Both schools were popular at the same time, yet Russell's canvas has an entirely different feel from the moralistic tone of the Pre-Raphaelites. *Alpes Maritimes* is alive with the freshness of morning and a hazy promise that is at once soothing and uplifting. Sulphur and white impasto shrubs appear to radiate, but so do the purple pools of shade beneath, and I am mystified by this.

Until I discover the secret: colour complementarity. If you stare at a yellow Post-It, then transfer your gaze to a white sheet of paper, a purple replica magically appears like an aura on the page. Luminous and vibrant, it is the precise shade raining down on me now in a jacaranda blessing. I remember the first time I experienced its effects, not then knowing that I did. It was on one of those rare occasions when a major international exhibition came to the Art Gallery of Western Australia in Perth, in this case Monet. Of course, I had seen his haystack series in reproduction and never understood what all the fuss was about. But when I stood before those summer grainstacks, I was immobilised by the sheer physicality of their power. These haystacks, so like and yet unlike the ones I grew up with, emitted a gathering heat and brilliance that went beyond the thing itself. The left flank of each pyramid was a blaze of gold, its opposite asleep in purple. In the reproduction, if you cover the violet shadow with your hand, the sunlit side appears less bright. Uncover it, and the hayrick explodes with brilliance once more. I remember the canvas as enormous, but later discovered it was not.

So what were the Impressionists trying to capture? More than faithful reproduction, it was the effects of light in all its evanescent moods at different times of day and changing seasons. And more than that, it was, as Monet put it in the context of his haystack series, a desire to encapsulate, 'instantaneity especially the "enveloppe", the same light spreading everywhere …' In this he was driven 'by the need to realise what I feel', in other words what he called 'sensation' or inner feeling,[3] and purple plays a vital role in this. For Johannes Itten, who taught at the Weimar Bauhaus with Kandinsky in the early 1900s, the tension between purple (as a cooler, secondary tone) and primary yellow creates an ethereal effect that transcends form.[4] This dynamic also evokes a sense of movement,[5] and for Monet, who speaks of light as Truth, this dance is as much an inner as an outer one.

The physics of colour was not understood until 1704 when Newton experimented by passing sunlight through a prism. Studying the resultant spectrum, he was struck by the absence of purple, so abundant in nature. By overlapping opposite ends of two spectra, however, he succeeded in generating 'extraspectral purple',[6] a term I like for its otherworldly resonance. It also accords with my take on purple as a liminal shade and threshold between worlds. It was the colour of the velvet cloth wrapped around the book of koans my Zen teacher would uncover when gifting me the next conundrum to wrestle with in meditation, a koan in the Japanese tradition being a word or phrase to contemplate on the way to enlightenment. These are threshold words designed to take you from the world of everyday things into the essential nature behind them. The book was called *The Gateless Gate.* I remember the womb-like feel of the room with its diminutive Buddha and mauve lisianthus cast like genies in a candlelit forest. And the grief of my disintegrating marriage contained by the poetry and pain of each koan as it bled into my life: *Mountains and valleys are different, the moon and the clouds are the same.* And all felt strangely blessed.

For the Impressionists, purple was such a mediator between light and the world of objects, or form. Itten, one of the last colour theorists to write on the dynamic interplay of colour, states: 'Colors are the children of light, and light is their mother. Light, that first phenomenon of the world, reveals to us the spirit and living soul of the world through colors.'[7] Artist and colour therapist Liane Collot d'Herbois similarly describes violet as a bridge between the physical and spiritual,[8] between object and essence. One image from the Melbourne exhibition that demonstrates this with particular poignancy is that of Mrs Russell amid a florescence of colour in the garden at Belle-Île. With her golden hair framed against a bank of purple cloud, it seems to presage her untimely death, the violet tones of the sky echoed in floral shadows below.

Goethe, whose *Theory of Colours* (1810) influenced Itten, d'Herbois and the Impressionists themselves, classifies the violet-purple spectrum as 'unnecessary',[9] which is disappointing coming from a poet and philosopher. Even the physicist Newton saw colours as vibrations like the seven notes on the musical scale,[10] and I have read that purple translates to C, B sharp.[11] Something I could have verified, if I'd ever thought to ask, with the synaesthetic Zen teacher who had a penchant for ruined pianos. Personally, I don't hold with Goethe when it comes to purple. To me, it is vital, and there are days when nothing else will do; when red feels too abrasive, blue too distant and cool; then I reach for purple to contain and uplift with its paradox of lightness and depth.

My purple coming of age was that first pair of bell-bottoms immortalised in a photo my boyfriend Pete took when he visited me in France. There I am – a heliotrope splash amid waist-high, pink-tipped grass, gazing into the valley mist of a small chateau. All suitably impressionistic, thanks to the blurred effects of the Kodak Instamatic. It is a colour I associate with Pete for his trademark purple jeans, a permanent fixture in university days, often worn with the rose damask shirt or white tracksuit top. There I am at eighteen perched on the handlebars of his bike, those plum-coloured legs angling in and out of my vision as we wobble along Aberystwyth Prom. I picture us, an oasis of colour beneath Welsh slate roofs and glowering skies, breaching puddles thrown by a steely sea. We sing 'Raindrops are falling on my head … crying's not for me …' and think we are invincible. I marry him, of course.

And I have had my own Mauve Decades, albeit measured out in months, when its variety of shades sustained me through motherhood and illness, marriage breakdown and divorce. Particular favourites were the purple cords and matching two-tone jumper purchased in haste when Simon had nodded off in the pram. It was ideal: warm, vibrant and fashionably 'cool'; it detracted from that sleep-deprived, harassed mother-of-two look, lending a deceptive glow to my skin. It nourished me, so that I in turn could nurture and love. I have a vivid memory of this outfit, worn for the last time on holiday in Wales when Simon was four. There I am lying in a hollow on the slippery Welsh grass under a sparse tree in weak sun, resplendent in purple. A remembered moment of deep peace I return to during relaxation after yoga, or whenever I need to centre myself.

The Impressionists took to mauveine with characteristic aplomb, yet also experimented with other new chemical dyes like magenta and solferino, both named after Italian battles, reflecting the turbulence of the period. These came on the market in 1860 and are evident in Russell's *Alpes Maritimes* as variants of gold and mauve. More hues followed, outstripping any modern-day Dulux chart for fanciful nomenclature; 'excited-thigh-of-nymph pink', for example, and 'caca Dauphin', which I venture to translate as 'Prince Regent poo'.[12] But I digress ...

The Impressionist revolution was through the medium of colour, breaking with the prescriptive use of dark earth tones and pale contrast espoused by the Académie Royale to embrace the full colour spectrum. Theirs was a rebellion against the formulaic imperative of idealised subject matter and form derived from mythological, religious and classical texts. Rather than reconstruct from memory in the studio, they worked outdoors, *en plein air,* the better to absorb the capricious moods of nature, and purple is key in capturing the atmospherics of light and distance, heat haze and mist. From the NGV exhibition, Russell's and Monet's *Belle* series are memorable, their shimmering purple-mauves combining with green and white to convey sea spray, lichen rock and that cool northern light. Viewed side by side, the influence of the older man on the young Russell is evident, and the effect is subtle, but real, as though I too am out in the open, far from a Melbourne gallery.

More than a school, the Impressionist movement was a state of mind, diametrically opposed to the black and white, chiaroscuro mentality of the established order which was now being challenged in the wake of the Industrial Revolution by the rise of a new middle class. The Impressionists applied colours directly and in juxtaposition to *suggest* rather than dictate form, sculpting shape with paint. The effect is to engage the beholder, not just optically as colours blend on the back of the retina, but also emotionally as we receive the 'sensation' or feeling behind the work; the essence that moved the artist to engage with the scene. Oils were layered in thick, deft strokes of broken hue to meet the moment, with no attempt to conceal brushwork. The results were considered shocking, and the artists often condemned as careless, puerile or mad.

The Impressionists were not bound by colour theory, even though they were influenced by it, for theirs was an intuitive aesthetic, affording them the liberty of discovery through experimentation. Pete and I tried this along with our two boys after enrolling them in the Steiner school. Like the Impressionists, Rudolf Steiner was a follower of Goethe and his ideas on the psychology of colour. So, there we are, the four of us, Pete, the children and I, seated on Goldilocks chairs at a baby-bear table splashing primary colours onto thick wet paper. Yellow is my colour of choice, which apparently means I'm sanguine – light-hearted and easily distracted. Pete is red, of course – choleric, and a bold man of action. Simon, too, is red, and Francis blue – the ever-thoughtful melancholic. Chasing instinct, I daub on sunshine paint, watching as the feathery fingers creep towards the corners, not quite filling the space like Pete's, and later drying out in a pallid blur. I try again, converting to blue, but in each case never quite resolve that tension between surrender and control.

My Zen teacher once described this in a meditation context as trying to ride an unbridled horse, mounting first this way, then the other and falling off anyway. Which is exactly how it felt in that tiny room with the swaying Buddha as I struggled to demonstrate my insight: *the sound of one hand, the mountains, the valleys – all different and the same.*

One of the paintings that stands out in my mind from the Melbourne exhibition is Russell's *The Garden, Longpré-les-Corps-Saints* (1887), depicting spring trees in bloom. Overwhelming in size and luminosity, its branches stream upwards and away beyond the canvas, the mauve blossoms of the foreground backlit by splashes of gold that could be foliage or light, and impressionistically both. Purple shadows on the central trunk are echoed in the garden wall and lithe silhouettes of distant trees, the whole contained within green and mauve undergrowth and a patch of celadon sky. Mauve petals tumble from the tree like firecrackers and my heart expands. So, *this* is how it feels to ride the horse! It brings tears to my eyes.

Russell knew only too well that painful tension between subjective expression and close observation of a reality ever in flux. Along with fellow artists Monet and Van Gogh, he was drawn to oriental philosophy, recognising kindred spirits in the Japanese artists of the *ukiyo-e*, or floating world, school who burst onto the scene in 1867 at the Universal Exposition in Paris.[13] Theirs was no lofty vision of an afterlife or the heroism of battle, no romantic idyll or mythological fantasy, but the depiction of the here and now. What in Zen terms is encapsulated in the act of chopping wood and carrying water as enlightenment itself. Here for the first time were artists showing ordinary people in the natural world of mountains and water, flowers and trees.

Monet was particularly enamoured of Hokusai (1760–1849), acquiring six of his famous woodblock series depicting Mount Fuji at different angles, seasons and times of day. He studied the *ukiyo-e* style down to brushstroke details and colouration, including the use of cool and warm colour contrast to suggest the play of light, atmosphere and mood, a dynamic, according to Itten, capable of transcending form.

For Monet, and Russell who was influenced by him, yellow and purple were their contrast twins of choice, the latter being especially prominent in the later works of Monet's lily pond series. Many of these paintings are awash with mauve to the extent that he has been suspected of having ultraviolet vision. When I first read this, I was intrigued but sceptical, until I heard an interview on ABC Radio National's Science Show with physicist Helen Czerski who confirms that the all-pervasive purple blush in Monet's later works – ostensibly those enormous water lily canvases – faithfully represents the world as seen through an ultraviolet lens. Or no lens, in Monet's case, who at the age of eighty-three had it removed from his right eye in a cataract operation. True scientist-cum-artist that he was, Monet resumed his colour experimentation, painting the same water lily scenes, first with a (cataract-ridden) left-eye view of reds, yellows and browns, and then in a striking dance of purple, mauve and violet through his ultraviolet right.

Apart from the haystacks, Monet's ultraviolet lily ponds are the works of art that continue to reverberate in memory long after that WA exhibition all those years ago. What is lost in reproduction, apart from their size – reaching from top to bottom of the gallery walls and equal in width – is their sheer vitality and presence. Viewed from a platform with a hundred other visitors, my gaze fell into purple watery depths, reflecting willow fronds and drifting cloud, the whole studded with the budding yellow counterpoint of *Hemerocallis* lilies.[14] Even in that crowded room, it took my breath away, and perhaps only now do I understand the enormity of its impact: to glimpse momentarily another way of being on the periphery of light.

Bruised – Jacqueline Wright

bruise /bruz/ *v.* **(bruised, bruising)** – *v.t.* **1.** to injure by striking or pressing, without breaking the skin or drawing blood. **2.** to damage (fruit, etc.) by applying pressure, without breaking the skin. **3.** to injure or hurt superficially; *to bruise a person's feelings.* **4.** to crush (drugs or food) by beating or pounding. **5.** to scratch or mark the surface of (leather or rock) usually for decoration. – *v.i.* **6.** to develop a discoloured spot on the skin as a result of a blow, fall, etc. – *n.* **7.** an injury due to bruising or contusion. **8.** a damaged area on a piece of fruit, etc., due to bruising [... ME, from OE *brysan* crush]
Macquarie Dictionary

Only a few months after he told me, I was cycling home from a friend's place when I hit the curb and flew over the handlebars. I don't know if it was the wine, or my bike light not working, but in the morning, I was all sorts of sore. A bruise budded on my thigh. Throughout the week, it spread around my upper leg and down to my knee, pinking then purpling. Then it did this amazing retro thing with mustard yellow. I didn't cover that bruise. Instead, I wore it like a medal. In my short denim skirt, I showed that bruise off. It instigated sharp, sucked-in breath and comments like, 'J-eee-zhas, Jacq, what happened?' People reached out to touch it but drew back. I was proud of that bruise and, for a long time after, I wondered why.

Now I know. To me, that bruise represented the internal bruise I'd suffered when my husband of eighteen years told me that he didn't love me anymore. No one can see those kinds of bruises. You carry them around inside you and knock them against the hard edges of life. Jim and I had been spending some time apart –

a 'trial separation' the psych called it. I was trying to make a decision. My husband was not going to change. Could I live with that and practice ongoing acceptance? If I couldn't, it was time to leave and move on. She made it sound easy.

*

We meet after sunset at Cable Beach foreshore. It is a blood-orange sky and the lighthouse to the south strikes a flash-pulse that matches one out of every ten of my heartbeats. I sit side-saddle on the railing, back to the beach, swinging my foot. Jim straddles the railing like it's a horse. I take a deep breath and say, 'I can't make a decision until I know where I stand. My feeling is that you don't love me anymore.'

Jim is unusually quick in his response. 'Yep,' he says, 'that about sums it up.'

Ouch! Striking without breaking the skin or drawing blood. Bruise, right? Big bloody bruise.

I paraphrase the whole thing again just to make sure he hasn't misunderstood the question, but nope, he got it right the first time. He lists reasons that seem so flimsy and unsubstantial. I listen and the foot that is attached to my leg keeps swinging while my world tumbles down around me.

Before he leaves he asks, 'Are you alright?'

'Sure,' I say in a small voice. It is all I can manage.

*

We all bruise. It's inevitable, isn't it, that people will bruise us. We know they will, because we've been bruisers ourselves. Girls are particularly good at landing blows on soft places with pointy words and deeds. I've been bruised by lots of people. Truth be told, I've done a lot of bruising back although I try hard, very hard nowadays to limit that. There's enough bruising being done in the world without me adding to it.

I used to think that some of us are like mangoes and bruise

easily, while others are of the potato variety and can take a bit of a pounding. It's a character-type thing. But my observations have revealed that we can morph from potatoes to mangoes, and vice-versa. Most of us develop tough skins at some stage in our lives. But there are times when we peel off our armour or allow people to get in. We expose our soft, squishy side to people we feel we can trust or people we want to trust. We thrust our vulnerability at them, whether they like it or not, and say, 'Here you go, welcome to the Inside Me.'

*

After Jim declared he didn't love me anymore, I went back to the place where I'd been boarding and played Scrabble with a friend. I put down a seven-letter word on the triple word score – 'bruised' – and scored a whopping eighty-three points. For about ten seconds, this made me feel better. Twenty seconds, when she assured me she wasn't going easy on me. Twenty seconds of not hurting at this stage of the separation game is good. Baby steps …

I tossed and turned that night. I got up with the sun and walked from the beach to the port. I shared my journey with a big dog that refused to 'Go Home!' Maybe it didn't have a home. In my sleep-deprived delirium I told myself that the dog was there to protect my heart, at which point, he took off into the dunes and I never saw him again. A small, stripey fish swam alongside me for the rest of the way and I made sure not to scare off this travelling companion by imposing grand titles on it like 'Heart Protector'.

I hitched a ride back home with a chopper pilot and we shared break-up stories. His wife had suffered from postnatal depression.

'I knew something was up when she said the sand was black,' he told me.

The birth was traumatic. In the middle of the night, she'd tapped him on the shoulder and told him it was time to go to hospital.

'"Yeah, yeah," I told her, "just like last time and seventeen hours later you had the baby. Wake me in the morning."'

She'd pointed to the baby's leg dangling from between her thighs.

'She screamed the bloody hospital down. They couldn't do a caesarean coz the baby was stuck in the birth canal, so they broke her pelvis to get him out.'

In the end, the doc unscrewed the forceps and used them like salad servers to dislodge the baby's head. They dislocated his shoulder to get him out and when he reached the outside world, he was purple. The doctor put the baby on his lap and tried giving it oxygen but, in all the confusion, the hose had been dislodged and oxygen was hissing unchecked from the bottle.

'I hooked it up, watched Mick turn pink and thought, finally, everything would be okay. A few months after, she said the sand was black and, you know what? Her mother fucking agreed. She patted her bloody hand and said, "Yes, darling, it is," and things were never right after that.'

He dropped me off at my driveway. With the car door open and the engine running, we talked some more.

'She left me with the kids and ran off with another bloke,' he said.

I asked him what helped soothe the bruising that comes with being left and unloved.

'Fishing,' he told me, without thinking. He shook my hand before driving away. 'Good luck,' he said.

It was like I was going into battle.

*

I tried sleeping again, without any luck, so I decided I'd tackle the mound of dirty washing. The place I was staying didn't have a machine. I'd made arrangements with a woman across the road that ran a B&B to wash my clothes. It took three visits.

When I arrived with the first load, Cathy asked me how I was going. I burst into tears and told her, 'Jim doesn't love me anymore.'

This prompted an eco cycle-long conversation.

'You know what, Jacq?' she finally asked as I piled the wet load into my basket.

'No,' I said, 'what's that?'

'At times like this I try and embrace the Buddhist concept of love. Do you know what that is?' She waited for me to stop and listen. 'Embrace the enemy. Wish them all the love that you would wish onto yourself.'

Through my mind flashed an image – me standing, feet planted, forearms crossed in front of my face, fists clenched.

'No deal!' I muttered out aloud, pegging up my first load. 'No deal!' All I could think of was how I wanted to bruise Jim back. Hurt him as much as he'd hurt me.

During my second visit to Cathy's washing machine, she asked again how I was going.

'Not great,' I told her. 'I've spent the last two hours crying.'

She looked at me. 'You know what, Jacq?'

'No,' I sniffed. 'What?'

'There are some people in the world that need to learn to cry more and there's others that need to cry less.'

On my last visit, Cathy caught me in the driveway trying to make a quick getaway with my coloureds.

'How you going, Jacq?' she asked.

'I only cried once!' I announced proudly.

'That won't last,' she shook her head. 'You'll go up and down and this will go on for years and years.'

*

I don't know why people talk about hearts breaking. The heart is a muscle, for Christ's sake, and muscles don't shatter. People can hurt us by retracting their love, or leaving us for others or just plain leaving us. But this is more of a bruising thing. Domestic violence, sexual and physical abuse, now that's a different thing. These actions have huge potential to inflict long-term psychological damage. They can break us and tear us apart. And the death of people you love. That's not bruising, either. Neither is grief a long-term illness. Like cancer, it ebbs and flows. Goes into remission. It comes back to bite us, often when we least expect it.

People like to give you advice when you split up. It ranges from quick fixes to long-term game plans. Over the next few months, I found most of it annoying, amusing and, on the whole, unsatisfying. The only advice I would pass on to The Bruised is: fish, stop listening to Leonard Cohen, and buy haemorrhoid cream. Listening to Leonard Cohen is like pushing down hard on your bruise. 'Wallowing' my mum would call it. Whatever you call it, it's not helpful. Fishing puts things in perspective: watching the tide go out dragged my angst into the open sea where it bobbed around small and insignificant. Haemorrhoid cream was more practical – it reduced the puffy eyes that came with constant crying. The advice I would give to Friends of The Bruised is to listen. That's all.

Other advice during that year was the *Getting Over It* school of thought. Like hurt was a hurdle. But I didn't believe that leaping over it and never looking back was going to work. There was also the school of *Toughen Up, Princess*. It's the sister school of *Tell Someone Who Gives a Shit*. It's a tough place, where I live, the North-West, but it's come a long way since I moved up here. We take our mental health a lot more seriously these days because of the high suicide rates. Everyone, particularly in Indigenous communities, is chalking up a suicide, or two or three, in their own family. Many of them are young men. Boys bruise too; it seems … not just on the footy field.

*

I became My Own Worst Enemy. Apart from going the knuckle on my bruise with Leonard Cohen, I kept a Bruise Inventory. Here are some of the items I listed:

- Bob Hawke discarding his long-suffering wife, Hazel, for his biographer, Blanche D'Alpuget.
- My friend's wife leaving him when she found out he had prostate cancer.
- Woody Allen falling in love with his adoptive daughter.
- Being texted by your long-term partner saying, 'It's over' and never seeing them again.

The purpose of the Bruise Inventory was to put my bruising in perspective. I tried to tell myself that what happened to me wasn't really up there with Bob taking off with Blanche.

*

As a result of falling into Cathy's crybaby category or administering too much haemorrhoid cream, I ended up with a persistent bloodshot eye, so I carted myself off to the doctor. He took my blood pressure. It was off the scale and he asked me if my life was any more stressful than usual. I burst in to tears and told him I was separating from my long-term partner. A child was involved. I left the surgery with scripts for conjunctivitis cream, anti-depressants and anti-anxiety tablets. I was also clutching a mental health care plan. He wouldn't give me a script for sleeping tablets. Yet sleep was the thing I most needed. The psych I'd been seeing was furious.

'Of course you're depressed and anxious. I'd be more alarmed if you didn't feel that way.'

She told me to only consider filling the prescriptions if I stopped eating, sleeping and being able to work.

'But call me before you go down that path.'

*

I didn't travel that path but I got pretty close. I stood at the beginning of the end of it, time and time again, unpacking my feelings in an attempt to understand things better. And it wasn't one path, I soon discovered, but many; the bitter and twisted one, the one that flogs you remorselessly, the trail of breadcrumbs leading to nowhere.

'Surely, surely,' I said to one of my Listening Friends, 'there's another way through this.'

'Maybe you're just not at a point in your life that you can imagine a happy ending,' he said. 'I'm the same.' He was a playwright and his strong point was satire ... plunge-the-knife-and-twist-it stuff. We both laughed unhappy laughs.

'He's right,' another Listening Friend said. I'd offered to help with the purging of her house. We'd got to the point of emptying out her built-in wardrobes and putting her junk into themed piles. We were just about to embark on the process of throwing away and delegation.

'Don't tell me there's no happy-ever-after,' I moaned, picking up a pile of stained linen, sandpaper bath towels, tea towels and placemats. I moved towards the op-shop box.

'No,' she said, plucking the pig of happiness tea towel from the top. 'He's right about the "imagining" bit.'

'You have a whole kitchen drawer stuffed full of tea towels,' I said, plucking it back.

'And you have chosen to see what happened in your life in one way, making up a story based on that one imagining.'

I threw the pile into the box and moved towards a stack of books and magazines.

'Being a writer, you should know that there are many ways to imagine or interpret an event,' she continued. 'You've just chosen this story to see things through a particular lens.'

'It's not about lenses. It's about bottom lines. You either love someone or you don't.'

'Wait,' she said rifling through the books I was about to cull. She plucked one with a cover straight out of the 70s, all swirling psychedelic pink and green. It was Alice Morgan's *What is*

Narrative Therapy? An Easy-to-read Introduction. It was thin, the cover flimsy and the only thing that got me opening it was the fact that Alice was Australian, not American.

I frowned as I leafed through the book, stopping at one page to read out aloud, 'The stories we make about our lives are created through linking certain events together in a particular sequence across a time period and finding a way of explaining or making sense of them … we have stories about ourselves, our abilities, our struggles, our competencies, our actions, our desires, our relationships, our work, our interests, our conquests, our achievements, our failures.'

'That's it.' My friend tossed a few old magazines into the op-shop box and put aside the *National Geographics*.

I pushed the mountain of clean washing to one side of the sofa.

'Keep it,' my friend said.

'I'll just read the first chapter,' I said, already absorbed, curling up. 'And don't think I didn't notice,' I muttered.

'Notice what?' she asked.

'That the pig tea towel made it back into the kitchen drawer.'

She returned the majority of piles back into the walk-in wardrobes while I read Alice Morgan cover to psychedelic cover.

*

After reading the book, I realised that I'd got so caught up in the story about my failure to make my relationship with Jim work that I'd shelved any stories I had about my achievements. How had my story as a gymnast in high school come to be an achievement story rather than a struggle story? Because I'd privileged medal-winning and praise when I'd mastered flips and dismounts. I'd overcome fear when I fell and kept on going. That's how.

During our lives, we live many stories at once. Sometimes they run parallel to each other but most of the time they layer-up and are multi-storied. Plot lines and themes shoot themselves into each other. They intertwine and are coloured by social and cultural values.

At certain times in our lives, particular stories gain precedence. Sometimes these stories may also become problem stories.

*

My son would give his right arm to be invisible but for me, my invisibility is an outstanding problem. I can be in a group of people and feel as if I am not being seen or heard by anyone. It has me thinking that I'm not important. My invisibility is magnetic, it attracts filings of lunch cancellations, unreturned telephone calls and not being invited to parties and camping trips. It renders me speechless or makes me say stupid things, it calls me 'dickhead', churns my guts, snorts at the way I deal with disagreements and, at times, has been known to relentlessly chant, 'B-o-r-ing! B-o-r-ing! B-o-r-ing!' Only recently have I named this 'invisibility'. Before that it was me being painfully shy and self-conscious. Naming it was powerful. It created a gap between 'me' and the 'problem'. Now I can see the problem for what it is.

Perspective is a wonderful thing. It creates a nice little lookout where I can stand and watch the problem's tricks and tactics, its rules, game plans, desires and, importantly, what forces are in league with it and the people in my life that cheer it on. I've learned a lot sitting at my lookout and watching. Not just about me, but about the huge part cultural and socio-political stories play in people's lives. Instead of seeing someone as 'lazy', for example, I can see how much credence Western society values hard workers and shuns idleness. Australia has a word for lazy people – 'bludgers'. At my lookout I can better identify these norms and this helps me to embrace and celebrate difference instead of categorising people in terms of how different they are from the accepted story. But it's a challenge, right? It's much easier to say someone is lazy and move on, rather than think about why we think they are lazy. When we call someone 'lazy', the person is the problem and the role social values play in this magically disappears. If I had ten bucks for every time I've heard a non-Aboriginal person call an Aboriginal person 'lazy', I'd be a rich woman. Yet Aboriginal people in the North-West put family above work and, instead of burning out, they tend to pace themselves, take time out to enjoy life and laugh.

*

Here is a story that begins in a Victorian primary school ground. A dog cocks its leg and pisses over the new girl's skirt. I take the new girl home where my mum sponges her skirt down with soap and warm water. They were hard days, I remember. Days of asphalt, grazed knees, taunts, teasing, corporal punishment and playground equipment that burned skin and broke bones. My friendship with Sarah Taylor and the pine forest surrounding the school were the only soft things available to me. Lying on a bed of brown, scented needles, we talked, laughed and shared secrets; but that all changed at high school. New friends found Sarah and her new friends didn't like me very much. That's when my problem story took over.

My Invisibility story consisted of one lonely lunch after another on the back step of a side entrance, far away from the netball courts, school oval and smokers' alley. Then, one lunchtime, my phys. ed. teacher, Carmel Morello, stopped to chat. Carmel Morello wore Adidas runners, skorts and those ankle socks with bobbles on the back. Her legs were smooth, muscular and tanned. She had a shiny, honey-brown bob, a cute up-turned top lip and dimples. Her cheeks were coloured and covered with that soft, peach-like fuzz. Lunchtimes together, when she was on duty, soon became a regular gig. We spoke mainly about gymnastics. She'd been a gymnast herself. We both loved Nadia Comaneci. Remember that sassy, young Romanian gymnast in the white leotard with the ponytail who made the double-tucked back salto executed from a handstand on the upper bar look like a walk in the park? After a month or so, Carmel Morello opened up the gym for me. I had it all to myself and tumbled around to my heart's desire. My story of Invisibility stopped being my main story. You know the rest.

But my Invisibility narrative is always lurking around on the sidelines. It recognises vulnerable moments and infiltrates its way into my life in insidious ways. I have learnt to be vigilant but also to tease it too. Problems possess us. They love seriousness. They get worried when you don't treat them with gravity. I can highly recommend laughing at problems.

*

When I first met Jim, I'd got sick of my former partner's fraternising and was living as a single mother with our preschool-aged son. I was amazed when the handsome, eligible bachelor on campus sat on my desk and asked me to take him camping at Easter. When he proposed to me, one year later, I didn't think to ask myself: Is this man right for me? Does he have the personality and the characteristics that I can grow old with? Are the things I like about him going to get us through those tough patches?

Instead, I turned to my Invisibility, gave it the forks and told it, 'See, you're wrong, I must be special and interesting.'

My giddy excitement at being valued blinded me to what was obvious to others, my mother especially. I'd overlooked the fact that the man I'd married did not put a high value on communication. We moved at a different pace to each other, rarely were we in time. And although we had a shared sense of humour and love for the underdog, our life priorities couldn't be more different. Sometimes this can work but in our case it didn't. His resentment and withdrawal added fuel to my problem story. I broke plates and hit out. And then it all ended up at Cable Beach with me swinging my leg and him telling me he didn't love me anymore.

*

I am thrilled when people take themselves out of the pigeonhole I've put them in and plonk themselves somewhere else. Ecstatic when they divvy themselves up and put themselves into multiple pigeonholes. Better still, kick apart those pigeonholes altogether. It's these kinds of experiences that have built great characters in my writing. I have a character in my novel *Red Dirt Talking* whom I'm particularly fond of; his name is Maggot and he is a garbo. Maggot has tatts and dreadies. He philosophises. He speaks eloquently, quotes poetry and is widely read. Some readers say to me that Maggot is an 'unbelievable' character. My response? 'Truth is stranger than fiction.' I've filled notebooks as testimony to that saying.

*

The other day, I had coffee with my friend who finds it hard to chuck stuff out.

'You look happier,' she observed. 'Lighter.'

I told her I had became less wrapped up in why Jim didn't love me and was focusing more on who did love me and why. 'I feel like I've moved the goalposts and changed the relationship I have with that particular problem.'

She knew what I meant. She'd been going through a bit of shit herself and we often talk about how hard it is to change the way you look at things and stop thinking of yourself as a certain type of person.

*

Bruises fade with time. Nowadays I've ditched the Bruise Inventory and become a love-story bowerbird. Not love between people because that's been done to death, but stories about things that sustain people when the people in their lives let them down or don't meet their expectations. Here's the beginning of mine:

> This love story happens in the steamy tropics. It involves fruit and a certain degree of flexibility but it's not what you think …

That's as far as I got, but basically it's set during the months before I left the family home to begin the tumultuous decision-making process of leaving or staying with Jim. I was doing a weekly yoga class held on the deck of the local café. Every week I placed my mat in the same spot under a peach-mango tree. When I was supposed to be practising shavasana, I looked up into the leaves of that tree. I watched it flower, I observed a small, green dot form from the flower. The dot grew from a kidney shaped bean into a fully-fledged mango, bright tangerine with a rosy flush. At the end of my last class, the teacher picked the mango and gave it to me. I ate it for breakfast, threw the seed into the garden, packed the car and drove away.

The mango, like the tide, reminds me that people fall in and out of love and the world goes on regardless. Somehow, for me, this is comforting.

My Descent into Purple – Hanifa Deen

I live in Melbourne and most of my clothes are black. Wearing black is an unwritten law one doesn't easily put aside, especially in writing enclaves and other avant-garde circles where the inner-city suburbs of Carlton and Brunswick are home to black-clad warriors of every age. Black is also the literary establishment colour and although I rarely cross this hallowed threshold, or consider myself a paid-up member, I do my best to abide by the 'bylaws' of bookish circles and my adopted city. Add to this the absurdity of walking down the Paris-end of fashionable Collins Street without showing a predilection for black!

Ten years ago, when I first came to Melbourne, I eased into my new tribal colours without any shilly-shallying. Farewelling Perth's magnificent beaches, cotton clothes and deep suntans, I said *Guten Tag* to Melbourne's European-like autumns and winters. In Melbourne, black and I adopted one another; I felt reborn, although discreet touches of red, burgundy and purple were permitted to signify that I was not trapped in perpetual mourning and I never deserted my footy colours, remaining true blue to the irreconcilably ugly yellow and blues of my West Coast Eagles, in the good years – and the bad. But let's put black to bed for the time being.

*

Investigating my purple past in search of inspiration led me to recently conduct a wardrobe inventory. Patches of purple soon emerged: purple shoes and hats, mauve gloves, scarves and – the pièce de résistance – a magnificent aubergine-coloured, ankle-length woolly coat from the 70s. On top of the pile I reverently laid my most recent purple purchase, a hooded raincoat bought for five dollars from my local drycleaner who, after waiting six months for its absentee owner to return, eventually released it into my eager hands: a perfectly legal, if somewhat opportunistic transaction. So I slowly came to realise that a purple portfolio had been with me for years; purple lurking in the background, silent, regal and as enigmatic as purple should be. The evidence mounted that, once upon a time, I had made a pact with purple.

How had this come to pass, I wondered? How had this penchant for purple slowly dislodged the reds and burgundies that I was once so fond of and which, I hasten to assure any Muslim Urdu readers, had nothing to do with wine or 'booze' – although *Sharab* may sound like Shiraz to the uninitiated. Oh *haraam, haraam*!

*

Intoxication with certain colours, and snubbing others, enters women's lives from an early age. We begin to slowly understand the place of colour in our lives, and identify with certain pigments at our mother's knee. My mother used to dress me in pink when I was little and to this day I associate its tender tones with a lack of will, or independence; a certain passivity verging on sulkiness. As I grew older I came to despise pink and to this day I avoid pink. Pink seemed vague, weak and stood in contrast to my mother's steely will (forcing my straight black hair into ring curls was another of Mum's daily regimes). Mum abided by the rule that little girls wore pink and little boys blue – blue was bold, blue was strong – pink was gentle, pink was 'nice'.

I, on the other hand, felt uncomfortable in pink partly for reasons that I only came to understand later in life. Growing up in the days of the White Australia Policy meant I encountered politics and racism at an early age, long before I knew the meaning of the two words. Immigrants who looked too beige, brown or black, were not allowed into the country and this may have led me to subconsciously identify pink with 'whiteness'; a skin colour I never aspired to – we were a proud family of Pakistani-Punjabi origin on Dad's side and Kashmiri-Welsh on Mum's. Both my grandfathers had entered (legally, I hasten to add) in the 1890s before the doors closed in 1901. Dressing me in a dainty pink dress with pretty smocking, pink socks, and a shiny pink satin bow in my hair was not going to turn this little brown girl into a little white girl – never my mother's intention – she only wanted me to 'fit in', to look 'nice' at birthday parties and the like.

My mum armed me well for combat; I'd come home from the playground upset and she would comfort me. 'If the Prophet Jesus Christ wanted to enter this country, *they* wouldn't let him!' she would say. Hooray! Jesus was brown – just like me! I inherited Mum's sharp tongue and irreverent outlook and these two gifts I nurtured at a time in our history when terms like 'multiculturalism' and 'cultural diversity' were not part of the Australian lexicon.

Much later in life I came to a better understanding of the mother–daughter connection; that first binding relationship in a young girl's life that falters but never fades; where a daughter struggles to control her own life without losing her mother's love. Reading Nancy Friday's *My Mother, Myself,* explained certain tensions between my mother and me as I was growing up, even in the small matter of choosing colours.

Under a maternal dictatorship we have no 'free colour will', so to speak. As we mature, our preference for certain colours emerges and becomes linked to our identity – some may be subconscious like a yearning to disobey, break the rules, become independent while others are more obvious – let's not mince words here. Doesn't *vanity* play a role? Men do not suffer from this malady: this obsession to enhance one's appearance through the magic of colour, although I've been told that generation Y males are heading down the corridors of colour consciousness.

Looking back over time at the palette of colours I have selected as an act of free will, I now understand that my real rapprochement with purple began much later in life and really had little to do with purple as a feminist emblem. I'm not embarrassed to admit publicly, for the first time, that purple appealed to me because it suited my brown hair, complexion and eyes – yes, 'colour conceit' conveniently cloaked under the feminist 'ism', added to my library of other 'isms'. Although this may shock some readers, I admit, from the distance of this page, that I possess a shallow streak of egotism. In the past I was happy enough for sister feminists and passers-by to assume what they liked – and besides I was a 'bloody feminist' so did it really matter why I donned the purple?

For the moment, however, let me take a pause from purple as I return to an earlier period in my life where the lessons I learnt formed part of my personal self-help manual on 'How to Manage Difference in Ten Difficult Steps'.

*

In the early 1970s I set sail for exotic shores, places and people. I was heading for 'Europe'. I was youngish, smug and adventurous. Yes, *I* would stay overseas in a non-English speaking country and experience the life of a foreigner. Often I'd had a taste of that at home when sometimes asked, 'Where were you born?' or 'Hanifa is a lovely name – where does it come from?' 'I come from a desert country', I would answer, trying hard not to smirk, before adding with a theatrical flourish that I was born in Kalgoorlie, Western Australia. Now I sensed that, once outside Australia, this insider joke would no longer serve me.

For nearly a decade, my colour of choice – the shade that held deep political and emotional significance for me – was red: stark, startling, dramatic, socialist. All of this took place in what I think of as my 'German period'. 'Radical Red' took hold of me. One might say I was wed to red!

I had eventually made my way via Holland to West Germany where I taught English at the Moltke Gymnasium (high school) in Krefeld for eight years. My German students dubbed me 'Skippy' during the era of the television show of the same name. This happened in the years before German reunification, when two Germanys existed – West Germany and East Germany, separated by the Berlin Wall.

I stood out: a foreigner who looked Turkish to most Germans, and was often taken for a *Gastarbeiter* ('guest' or foreign worker). The term 'guest' made me smile for I knew that, like all visitors, you were always expected to one day pack up and leave.

Gastarbeiters carried out the work no right-minded German would do, and returned to Turkey or Spain a little richer but much wiser as to the ways of the West. *But that was in the bad old days.* Germany has changed over the last three decades since the two Germanys were reunited and citizenship laws reformed.[1] This is not the Germany I remember. In the 70s my own nationality and background were often questioned. English might be my mother tongue but I didn't look American or British in most people's eyes. Perhaps people were just curious, but I'd had a lifetime of answering this question … some were more than inquisitive.

What did I do for a living? Was I really a high school *Lehrerin*: teaching at an elite German school? I knew what they meant. I looked like a brown Turkish guest worker – maybe a *Putz Frau*, a cleaning lady – why masquerade as a teacher? They were signalling, politely, that I should know my place. All right! I might not look like a 'dinky-di Aussie', I decided, but doubting my professional credentials was beyond the pale.

> I am sitting with friends at a crowded local café when a man, listening in from an adjacent table, interrupts and proceeds to inform all and sundry that I, most certainly, am not an Australian! I'm a *Schwindler* (imposter, poseur). He's been to Sydney, he says, and Australians don't look like me.
>
> '*Wetten wer?*' I reply. (You want to bet?)
>
> Off I race in my red VW Beetle (dubbed 'Eric the Red')

returning fifteen minutes later, passport in hand, whereupon I take a 100 Deutschmark off him with a smile. If I remember, he was, more or less, a good loser. I knew my dad – staunchly Muslim, but in his younger days occasionally tempted to have a 'flutter' on the 'gee-gees' – would have been proud of me.

*

By then I belonged to a posse of outsiders comprised of non-Germans and 'naughty' Germans. The non-Germans were mainly from Turkey, Spain, Chile and Ecuador. I remember the Chilean male students – the guitar music they played, their mood-swings from laughter to melancholy, how they relived the overthrow of their elected Socialist President Allende by General Pinochet in 1973. The 1982 movie *Missing* based on the book of the same name by Thomas Hauser relates in detail what happened to three thousand Chileans. Two hundred thousand went into exile.

As for the 'naughty Germans', they were members of the Deutsche Kommunistische Partei. These were the folk who nurtured my ascent into 'redness'. In 1972 party members were trapped in a catch 22 legal paradox, the so-called 'Edict Against Radicals'.[2] The Communist Party might be legal under the constitution, so was their daily newspaper, but members of the party were *Berufsverbot* (forbidden) from working as teachers, social workers, and in other public sector jobs, and branded as 'the enemy within' – even a poor old 'town postie' was sacked. More than three million people were put through loyalty checks resulting in eleven thousand ban proceedings. Admittedly this was a reaction to the Red Army Faction terrorism at the time. Careers, marriages and lives were ruined.[3]

The red brigade and I got on well. They liked foreigners, displayed a droll sense of humour, were the 'full bottle' on international politics (albeit with a 'twist' of Lenin), opposed South Africa's apartheid policies and the Vietnam War; they were a collective of motivated journalists, actors and artists – altogether a loquacious lot and maybe a reflection of myself at the time. They were not as 'correct' as my teaching colleagues who, while friendly enough in the staff room, never invited me into their homes. With the latter I remained 'on the outside looking in'. So I became redder and redder: jackets, scarves, boots, my auto *Eric the Red* and more importantly a way of looking at the world that crossed borders of race and ethnicity. Social Justice was the rallying cry for the red posse I rode with.

*

At around this time I encountered my first red feminist heroine – Clara Zetkin. I'd never heard of her before. Originally a Socialist Party leader, she became a member of the new German Communist Party in 1919. Clara and her colleague, Luise Zietz, founded International Women's Day (IWD). More than a million women across Europe marched on March 19th, 1911. Why was her name missing from the books I'd read on feminists?

Almost overnight I morphed into a conspiratory theorist. As history shows, the second wave of Anglo-American feminism in the 70s carried the day: purple and green prevailed and won the tug of war against red; the latter becoming passé except in certain labour movements around the world where you can't keep a good Red down.

Today in the twenty-first century, there's room for everyone. IWD is a global phenomenon, albeit a rather commercialised Remembrance Day laden with lunches, speeches and twenty-four hour bonhomie. Modern histories now include Clara. I am content – Clara has emerged from 'exile'.

Non-conformity and defiance are traits that fascinate me perhaps more than they should. I associate them with history, politics, literature – and the wonderful world of cinema. I've been a movie buff practically all my life and used to wag grade seven primary school to sneak into picture shows (globite case in hand) and gaze enraptured at the big screen and the big stars. My parents and teachers never found out and of course I forged my mother's signature on notes to the teacher, claiming, 'poor Hanifa wasn't well yesterday ...' Sometimes I wonder if I'd not 'descended' into writing non-fiction, might I have written the odd (perhaps very odd!) screenplay? How do you define a feminist movie in the twenty-first century? *Thelma and Louise*, *The Colour Purple* – so many contenders – surely not 'chick flicks' – I hope not.

A screenplay about Clara that oozed box office appeal? Somehow I doubt it. Yet the material is all there even if the audience isn't! The closing scenes all based on a day in August 1932 ... not fiction but fact.

> *Physically frail, seventy-five-year-old Clara travels 1,000 miles by train from Moscow (where she now lives) to Berlin to claim her right, as the Reichstag oldest member, to open Parliament. Leaning on her walking stick, she denounces her old enemy, Paul von Hindenburg, President of the Weimar Republic. On that day SS troops wait outside shouting battle cries, demonstrating what is yet to come. A year later the way is clear for Hitler. Clara dies that same year.*

Wake up! Time for a reality check! Even if Clara was played by the ever-imperious Dame Maggie Smith, looking down her nose, ready to box ears and thump anyone in her way with a black ebony-handled walking stick, it would be a flop. Sixty or so years after the end of McCarthyism and the Un-American Activities Committee, I somehow doubt that Hollywood is ready for Lenin's voice-over at the end.

> 'The German Communists have only one good man and that is a woman: Clara Zetkin.'
> Music swells ... Camera fades ... credits run – and there's my name on the list. Curtain descends.

The road to purple was a long and winding road with rest stops along the way. Every few years, for a month or so, I left Germany and returned to my hometown Perth. To my surprise I found that hems were longer, a new 'ism' called 'multiculturalism' was hailed as a prestigious government policy and, following the end of the Vietnam War, South Vietnamese refugees (dubbed 'boat people') were settling in, plus – lo and behold – some women were keeping their maiden names after marriage. And long overdue changes in some aspects of Aboriginal affairs had begun – Land Rights in 1976. The Deaths in Custody Commission and the Australian Council for Aboriginal Reconciliation were yet to come.

On each visit I noticed the exciting development of the second wave of Australian feminists. These were heady times; I read one feminist book after the other …: I fell in love with Betty Friedan's *The Feminine Mystique,* Germaine Greer's *The Female Eunuch,* Anne Summer's *Damned Whores and God's Police,* Marilyn French and a host of others. I finally returned home for good in late 1979 and nearly drowned in the new wave of purple. Wearing purple became a statement, but the colour didn't move me emotionally. I ticked the box but worried that I was becoming an 'absentee feminist', just as I had once been an absentee Australian.

Dale Spender used to say, 'If someone says, "Oh, I'm not a feminist," I ask, "Why? What's your problem?" Spender, in the 1980s, began wearing purple in recognition of the early suffragettes and this rich colour now became 'ours'. But as I have already confessed, that is not why I befriended purple. In the 80s, Reclaim the Night marches and the colour purple took off with a vengeance. I joined the marches but not the organisations for two reasons: firstly, I felt Australian – I always had but saw no traces of me in these new organisations; secondly my energy and commitment was focused on the nascent migrant workers' movement and the emergence of ethnic communities' councils around Australia supporting the new policy of multiculturalism, which in those days was not a 'dirty' word. Multiculturalism to me meant more than applauding culinary exotica and smiling on Harmony Days. Harmony has never been one of my strengths; as a writer I am more interested in clarifying conflict. I smell conflict and I see red!

After a stimulating and unsteady career in the public service in the government bureaus of multiculturalism, equal opportunity and human rights, I grew weary of my *Yes Minister* style reports written in turgid prose that dulled the senses and should have led to my arrest for murdering the English language. Finally, I handed in my public service uniform of cream suits with padded shoulders, stocking tights and mini-heels and turned to full-time writing about people who were reflections of me and my family – my tribe in the good times – and the bad.

By the mid-1990s there were approximately 350,000 Muslims in Australia – the White Australia Policy was over. The vast majority of Australians looked at Muslims with indifference – the term 'Islamophobia' was not yet a part of Australian mainstream language. September 11, the Bali bombings, and other murderous outrages committed in the name of Islam would one day change this. Being ignored but nevertheless getting on with your life wasn't possible any more – mindsets hardened. Muslims became trapped in an age of circling the wagons, forced, or 'seduced' into constantly defending Islam. I took another way out: writing non-religious books about Muslims as people who mowed their lawns (or didn't), worried about losing weight or paying the mortgage, who fell in and out of love or told their kids bedtime stories.

*

On one of my many research trips to Bangladesh for my book *Broken Bangles,* I discovered so many reflections of myself that I grew dizzy. I felt completely at ease with the proliferation of women's groups run by sari-clad NGO workers; we adopted one another. They introduced me to a remarkable Bangladeshi feminist from the past, unknown to Western feminists – just like Clara – and another woman to add to my collection of feminists from other cultures and ideologies.

Begum Rokeya Hossain, more than a hundred years ago, created her own utopian vision in her 1905 satire *Sultana's Dream*. In a country called Ladyland women run the country: women are the politicians, the scientists, the soldiers and the traders. Where are the men? In Ladyland it's the men who languish on soft couches inside – the harem – in purdah – in total social isolation. Rokeya's husband, an unusually progressive man for the times, remarked on reading her story, 'What a splendid revenge!' Rokeya wrote her satire ten years before Charlotte Perkins Gilman's famous work, *Herland,* in 1915.

Three years ago, inspired by Rokeya's writing, and together with a small core group of Australian Muslim women, I began an online magazine written and produced by Australian Muslim feminists called *Sultana's Dream*.[4]

*

The story of women's struggle for equality belongs to no single feminist nor to any one organization but to the collective efforts of all who care about human rights.
Gloria Steinem

I have always admired disobedient women in history, literature and real life. There is something about being a disobedient woman that is intoxicating and liberating. Clara Z., Rosa Luxemburg, Begum Rokeya, Emmeline Pankhurst and the English suffragettes, the New York garment workers, Simone de Beauvoir, Scheherazade, Madame Bovary, Marie Curie, Miles Franklin, Germaine Greer, Gloria Steinem, Lena Horne, Nina Simone, Ingrid Bergman, Katharine Susannah Prichard. Disobedient women in real life, literature and on the screen, joined by a chorus of nameless, faceless women around the world who have rallied, marched, shouted, refusing to surrender to prejudice and the social shackles of the period in which they lived. I thank them all.

The latter decades of the twentieth century marked the epicentre of my own feminism but, using the language of the times, I don't think being a 'women's libber' ever meant being 'cool' or 'hip'. Neither was it 'fashionable' in the nineteenth century; risky – yes; unpopular – yes. Women rallied, in spite of being ostracised, knowing they needed numbers to win the right to vote, own property and the rights that men took for granted.

And in the twenty-first century – where are we now? Is the era of female empowerment over? Julia Gillard, as Australia's first female prime minister, would have something to say on the subject.

Feminism has a PR problem – but then it always has. The mantra 'No, I'm not a feminist, but …' I find tedious. Do we need a surge of celebrity feminists to make the 'f' word functional once again or more Dale Spenders asking 'Why not? What's your problem?' Reducing the number of weight loss articles in women's magazines, diluting recipes and trimming fashion promos is not going to happen. A petition banning the Kardashian family from social media and magazines may be doomed to failure – someone else just as embarrassingly puerile would step into the spotlight. Western women seem trapped between thinking they have it all, but knowing deep down that sexual harassment, discrimination, rape and family violence remain with us. Pay gaps between men and women today are no laughing matter – a woman earns less than eighty-two cents for every dollar a man earns.

*

I sometimes fantasise about having my own signature flag, my own identity icon, incorporating black, red and purple. Flying defiantly from my rooftop or (in more maudlin moments after an hour at the gym) draped over my coffin, my imagination plays with colours and what they mean to me. Perhaps it's just as well that I write non-fiction, for any attempts at fiction could easily lurch into the horror genre.

So here I shall nail my colours to the wall. Black, red and purple – my three identity colours – a colour testimonial of a kind. A last hurrah!

Why black? Because black makes me invisible; I become an observer, sitting in the corner noting the foibles of human behaviour. I watch silently. Black is the opposite of white! I need say no more. And I don't believe in surrender; black gives me licence to be dangerous, to feel like a literary anarchist – my pen is my bomb and I'd look good in a long black coat and a sinister-looking black hat … 'Catch me if you can!'

Red? Good old red! It helps me remember; serves as a radical and rebellious symbol of affiliations that do not die. I feel I belong to this group of dissenters – women and men; my membership has not lapsed. Red sometimes makes me feel a little bit blue when I look at the world and the conflicts and think that nothing has changed.

With purple I am a part of the twenty-first century; I step out of the wings, taking my place as an older woman: confident, irritating and a purple pain-in-the-arse. I am reminded of my purple-patch days; nostalgia settles in. Perhaps one has to reach a certain maturity before donning purple for its soul; its depth is quite overpowering. Purple lurking in the background sometimes forcing its way to the front, a reminder of all the disobedient women I have known and have yet to meet.

These three colours are my identity markers – my very own *tricolore*.

Vive la difference!

Towards Metamorphosis – Amanda Curtin

I started lying about my age in my mid-forties. It wasn't intentional, but whenever I was asked how old I was, I would say forty-four. Unthinkingly.

My GP frowned at my patient record one day and announced, in a disapproving voice, *Actually, Amanda, you're forty-eight*. I was genuinely shocked – not at being forty-eight (which was shocking enough) but at the unconscious externalisation of my disbelief that any number greater than forty-four could possibly relate to me.

As fifty approached, I felt compelled to do something to mark – if not celebrate – this milestone, to stare it in the face. I declared I would get a tattoo.

The inevitable question – *Why a tattoo?* – was hard to answer. Perhaps it was a nod to the teenage goth I probably would have been if goths had been around when I was a pallid sixteen-year-old with darkly gothic tastes. Perhaps it was just resistance to the idea of *growing old gracefully*. It felt like a promise to myself, written on the skin. A rejection of the stasis of *forever forty-four*. Possibility. Hope.

It wasn't until I had committed to the tattoo, when I had chosen my self-inscription, that I could put a word to all of this: metamorphosis.

*

The world is full of metamorphosing older women. A cheese plate taught me that.

The cheese plate in question was a gift my friend Pat received for a significant birthday. Brightly painted, it came with a matching knife, the shape of which confirmed that, despite appearances to the contrary, the plate and knife were indeed meant for cheese.

There was nothing cheese-related about the image on the plate – no wedges of Swiss, rounds of cheddar, a pear or an apple or a bunch of grapes. Instead, there were three glamorous women wearing wide-brimmed hats trimmed with roses. (Even now I wonder about the association of those women with *cheese*.)

I didn't understand the significance of the gift until Pat showed me the poem that had come with it – 'Warning' by Jenny Joseph[1] – and I realised that the colours the cheese-plate women were wearing were red and purple.

Jenny Joseph's poem has become a rallying cry for many women coyly referred to as *of a certain age*. In a deceptively quiet, sedate voice, the poem's narrator speaks of what she will do when she is 'an old woman', which amounts to relinquishing the sober, conventional behaviour of the younger self who pays the rent, doesn't swear, sets a good example. The old woman the poet aspires to be is delightfully extravagant, bloody-minded, spontaneous and individualistic – spending her pension on brandy and summer gloves, eating whatever she wants, learning to spit. And the image in the poem that has come to be associated with the old woman's raft of subversive behaviours is the wearing of a purple dress with a red hat, regardless of the clashing colours, regardless of suitability.

The poem ends with the narrator musing over whether she should start behaving a little more like her older self now, so as not to shock people later – a suggestion (indeed, a *warning*, as the title tells us) that her present responsible self is only a veneer, and the flamboyant woman within might break free at any moment.

The women decorating my friend's cheese plate were not an especially fitting representation of the poem's wickedly defiant old woman, but this was a gift given, and received, in an acknowledgment of her spirit, and intended as a celebration of growing older as a positive experience – as a process of *becoming*.

*

That *becoming* works both ways cannot be denied. Here's a fundamental negative: 'For ageing women, invisibility is both a feeling and a reality, and the silence of not being addressed is deafening.'[2]

It's a given that women over fifty are socially invisible. On the net you can find any number of articles attesting to this. Many of them especially bemoan the loss of visibility to men. Apparently (and my learned source is the *Oprah Magazine*), it is Darwinian. Men are biologically programmed to notice only women young enough to bear them children, shoring up the future of their genetic imprint.[3]

But this doesn't explain the blinkered gaze of younger women.

A common scenario for women my age: you're at the counter of a newsagency, waiting to pay, your packet of envelopes in one hand and your cash in the other. The young assistant, female, serves two people before you, and you are patient – anyone can make a mistake – but when it happens for a third time you speak up.

Oh, sorry, she says, genuinely surprised at your apparent materialisation in front of her eyes. *I didn't see you.*

I have a theory that when young women 'don't see' older women, they are unconsciously closing their eyes to the fleshly proof that their youth is not forever. The 'not seeing' is literal. But it's a metaphor, too, for something more wide-ranging and disturbing: fear of social dismissal. 'To grow old as a woman in Western society is to become devalued.'[4]

There's a chasm between being invisible and being written off.

In my experience, the only perspective from which visibility actually increases as a woman grows older is the institutional. Within a week of turning fifty, I had received an appointment from the Department of Health's BreastScreen program, and an invitation involving nasty little sticks and sample containers from the National Bowel Cancer Screening Program. While I applaud these screening programs that help save lives, I was unnerved by the sensation that I had suddenly become a body in need of surveillance. And don't get me started on the letter I received from a geriatric research team inviting me to participate in a study on depression among 'older Australians still living in their own homes'.

Hilary Mantel observes that in the time and place of her childhood, women over fifty were not invisible; in fact, they were so sturdily visible that they 'blacked out the sky' and ruled the world. I love Mantel's suggestion that we revive the spirit of these women, who were 'unyielding, undaunted and savagely unimpressed by anything the world could do to them'.[5]

To be 'savagely unimpressed' – now, that seems something admirable for an invisible woman to aspire to.

*

My friend's cheese plate made retrospective sense of something I'd seen years before in the city of Perth: a lunchtime army of women wearing purple dresses and red hats.

It was like a loosely interpreted uniform, consistent in colour but not in expression. Some had chosen long and flowing purple; some, tailored; others, raceday purple with frills. And there were hats of straw and hats of silk, embellishments of net and bows and beads and flowers.

The other element of the uniform appeared to be laughter: loud, uninhibited, in-your-face.

I now know they were members of a worldwide movement inspired by Jenny Joseph's poem and aimed at making 'invisible' older women impossible to miss. Red-hatters, as they are often called, are women aged fifty and over who meet in public for social outings, dressed in their own interpretation of purple and red.

Red-hat groups have few rules. Members are not obliged to engage in good works or onerous committee duties; they are not, in fact, obliged to do anything.[6]

I began to wonder about these thousands of red-hatting women. Their obvious motivation was to reclaim their visibility in the world. But were they also expressing something that was the equivalent of my tattoo?

In the studies and stories I read, it appeared that, for many red-hatters, the main attraction *was* being the centre of attention: 'You wouldn't believe the amount of attention we get',[7] 'It is amazing that when you put a red hat on, the people that notice you, the men that will talk to you'.[8] Some said that being a red-hatter made them feel younger, more confident, more important.[9]

However, 'having fun' and 'being silly' seemed to be prized above all else:

> I don't have to prove myself anymore ... I just want to do fun things.[10]

> When we get on our purple and our red, we're allowed to be silly ...[11]

Red-hat groups say that while the focus is on fun, they also fulfil a valuable social function, providing avenues for socialisation and friendship among women who have lost partners, friends, work, purpose.[12] And the collective 'don't care' attitude certainly works against stereotypes of the older woman selflessly devoting herself to others while fading away into beige or pastel oblivion.

But there are contradictions in the philosophy underlying red-hatting, as a US study points out. On the one hand, the movement challenges ageist attitudes and limiting gender roles, by encouraging women to be self-focused, loud, visible and 'unladylike'; on the other, it supports the conventional and the traditional by encouraging 'the ladies' to dress for the male gaze in hyper-feminine attire.[13]

Either way, I couldn't see the seed of my own nebulous notion of *becoming* here.

The popularity of red-hatting seems to be declining in some places, with groups disbanding, having lost their enthusiasm for 'dressing up in the garb and all that'.[14] And I found some trenchant critics.

'Elderblogger' Ronni Bennett wrote of feeling discouraged 'that so many older women are organized for such a shallow objective.'[15] Comments on her blog post ranged from women defending red-hat ideals to those just as critical of them:

> Wearing that stuff is like donning a uniform, but without any real meaning or purpose.
>
> ... it made me think of teenage girls all being unconventional in exactly the same way.[16]

Like, say, goths?

I asked my friend who had received the cheese plate bedecked with red and purple ladies whether she had ever been tempted to become a red-hatter. She was polite but firm: *I have nothing against it. It's just not for me.*

*

> Within the dominant colour system of the modern west, older women's dress is associated with muted, dull, soft colours like beige, grey, lilac and navy-blue ... [This] relates to the more general practice of 'toning down' ... Purple is an ambivalent colour, associated with royalty and gorgeousness, but also vulgarity and coarseness. In emphasising this colour, Joseph's poem encapsulated the resistance to demands to tone down behaviour and dress, and to become grey and invisible.[17]

I have always been that person who admires bright, beautiful colours in a shop window and then asks the assistant, *Does it come in black?* (See? Closet goth.) But last year my friend Wendy gave me a gorgeous purple silk scarf to celebrate the publication of *Elemental* (which features such a scarf), and on a whim I bought a dress in the same colour. This out-of-character purchase was not a grab for attention in the style of the red-hatters – but ...

You know, in retrospect, I *should* have asked whether it came in black.

*

Let me tell you a story about a failure to metamorphose.

The 2014 Perth International Arts Festival (PIAF) featured Israeli-based Batsheva Dance Company's *Deca Dance* – ten pieces drawn from choreographer Ohad Naharin's twenty-year repertoire.

I wish I'd been able to watch all ten pieces. But I missed one, and I saw one of the others in the most superficial way because by then I was in a state of shock – physical, adrenaline-fuelled shock.

Attending *Deca Dance* had been a last-minute decision, and I went alone, thrilled to have scored a single seat about ten rows from the stage and just off centre. From the beginning, it was spectacular, the choreography startling, the energy and artistry of the eighteen dancers electrifying.

And then ... and then ...

Here is an extract from a review of *Deca Dance* – not of the performance I went to but of the same show performed at the New Zealand Festival a few weeks later:

> One excerpt was understandably the audience's favourite and mine too. Dressed in slick black suits and fedoras, the dancers slowly left the stage and coolly selected members of the audience ... Back on stage, however, the coolness disappeared and the party began.
>
> Not once were the participants put down or ridiculed by the dancers, as so often is the norm in this kind of interaction. At the close of the piece, everyone dropped to the floor, leaving one couple dancing in close embrace.

> Then suddenly the male dancer hit the floor as well, leaving the lone woman happy to take her well-deserved ovation.[18]

Now, this review requires a little insider deconstruction because, as you have probably guessed, I am intimately acquainted with the experience of that *lone woman*.

You've seen those wildlife documentaries where a lion surveys a herd of gazelle from the sidelines and you know, you just *know*, it's going to be that poor scraggly thing at the back that it chooses. I'm here to tell you that it doesn't do for the scraggly one in the middle to be complacent, either.

I was the last, that night, to be *coolly selected*.

Like everyone else, I had turned in my seat to watch as the dancers left the stage and roamed the aisles, searching, selecting. I wasn't on the end of a row; I felt safe.

And then I became aware of a frisson of movement to my right. I heard gasps. I glanced around. There was a dark, lithe figure inching along my row from the side. At that point, I began to mutter: *Not me, not me, please not me.*

Alas…

On stage my stern, cool partner morphed into a riotous headbanger, like the other dancers and the women from the audience they had led up on stage, and so in the spirit of okay-there's-clearly-no-getting-out-of-this and what-the-hey-it-will-be-over-before-you-know-it, I flung myself around a bit. For a whole song. And then, thank the universe, the music stopped, people cheered, and it was done, right?

No.

A Broadway song began, but the professional dancers were into their routine now and nothing seemed to be required of the amateurs other than to stand there and watch (and marvel – those dancers were *amazing*). I also looked around surreptitiously for the nearest exit off the stage. But there was to be no quick exit for me.

The Broadway song segued into a cha-cha, and what little participation was demanded of me I managed (except for the bit when the poor man tried to lift me; I whispered, *You. Have. Got. To. Be. Kidding.*).

Note, please, that by now I had been up there for *three songs*.

What relief when the track finished and the dancers led us to the front of the stage to bow. Even when another song began, I remained elated because it really did seem to be over. The amateurs were being led off the stage to the left, to the right.

Unfortunately, I was not going anywhere.

Despite my politely desperate gesturing that we follow the others, my partner and I were still centrestage, dancing to that execrable song 'Sway', and he, undaunted by the previous futile effort, was still occasionally trying to lift me.

Eventually, as the reviewer reports, all the professional dancers dramatically hit the floor as though shot. But was this lone woman *happy to take her well-deserved ovation*? I took mine swiftly and fled.

Finding yourself on the stage of the State Theatre is a surreal experience. All you can see is lights. But you can hear, by the laughter, that there are more than a thousand people out there, witnessing your gazelle-in-the-headlights, get-me-out-of-here, I'll-do-anything-you-want-just-make-this-end-*now* anti-performance.

You might be wondering whether I can dance. Well, actually I could, once. As a child. The twelve-year-old me even represented Western Australia in national ballroom dancing championships. (I disclose this only to gratify my mother, who is inordinately proud of it.) But I retired soon after. It was long ago. People write historical fiction about that decade.

Now I have middle-aged feet. I have had spinal surgery. I am impossibly uncoordinated. Other than a couple of forays into bellydancing and Bollywood – for fitness, and in the privacy of my own home – I have left dancing to dancers.

So, in effect: no, I can't dance. Whatever atavistic dance memory remains in my cells, it wasn't enough.

Here's a list of things I wish I hadn't worn on my night out to see *Deca Dance*:

1. orthopaedic sandals
2. leggings, which tend (I *now* know) to creep uncomfortably south in situations of vigorous movement
3. a pedometer, attached to said leggings (I was on the 2/5 diet and counting steps – and the fact that the pedometer was shocked into arrest speaks volumes, I feel).

But most of all, I wish I hadn't worn that purple dress and the beautiful purple scarf Wendy gave me. Why? Well.

When I got home from the theatre that night, I told my husband what had befallen me. (He tried admirably not to snort.) Then I held my breath for an hour or so. If anyone I knew had been in the audience, they would have been on the phone to have their guffaw. Nothing.

But a few weeks later, at the opening party of the Perth Writers Festival, I was introduced to the Director of PIAF, Jonathon Holloway, who frowned a moment before exclaiming, *I know! Yes! I saw you at the State Theatre…* etc. etc. *Hahahaha…* etc. etc. And he said he'd seen *Deca Dance* performed several times in different cities – *and they always choose someone colourful as the lone woman*. Apparently, there was even a purple spotlight pooling on me in my dying moments.

*

It would have made a good story, wouldn't it, if I had suddenly reconnected with my twelve-year-old dancing self on the stage of the State Theatre and (as they say) torn up the floor. If my orthopaedic sandals had miraculously turned into stilettos and my feet been refashioned to suit. If I had metamorphosed into some gorgeous creature able to make the stage her own and to hell with it, to dance like no one was watching, to become, at fifty-six, the centre of attention *and loving it!* That's what Jenny Joseph's wicked narrator would have done. And probably the red-hatting women, too.

I failed on all counts. And so I have to wonder: if I am in the process of becoming, then *what is it* that I am becoming?

Sometimes the only way to answer *what is it?* is to eliminate all the *what-it-is-not*s.

I'm not seeking the kind of visibility that makes me the centre of attention – unless I'm meant to be because I'm reading or teaching or speaking publicly as part of my work as a writer. (Really, I would have made a hopeless goth.)

I'm not harbouring an outrageously flamboyant self who longs to break free and fling herself into the purple spotlight; I've always been a quiet observer and am happy to remain that way.

I don't feel bereft at no longer being an object of the male gaze. But nor do I wish to be rendered socially colourless – unseen, obsolete, dismissed.

It's unlikely I will ever attain the heights of being savagely unimpressed with what the world does to me, although I remain resolutely admiring of those who are.

I don't yearn to spit or be silly, or to wear a uniform of red and purple. In the words of my friend: it's just not for me.

But I am way past forty-four now, and in order to own the age I am and accept all those other numbers yet to come, I need to believe that, in growing older, the focus might be on the *growing*. That change need not be only about degeneration and loss. That I might have more to offer than the statistics to be gained from scans and sample jars bearing my name. What ordinary, human needs they are.

These words from William Yeoman in *The West Australian* resonate with me:

> The sense of possibility in the midst of our always-becoming selves is the ultimate source of all hope, and of all creativity. The first step is recognising our real, imperfect selves and not our imagined selves, whether good or bad, and move from there.[19]

What is it I am becoming? I think it's okay not to know. Perhaps the *point* is that we don't.

Ironically, the tattoo I chose for my mark of resistance is remarkable among tattoos only for its utter conventionality. But I love the butterfly on my ankle.

Just as ironically, in spite of my wanting goth-black, it turned out a little bit purple.

Notes and References

Introduction

John Edmonds, *Tyrian or Imperial Purple Dye: The Mystery of Imperial Purple Dye*, Historic Dye Series, John Edmonds, UK, 2000.
Elisabeth West FitzHugh and Lynda A. Zycherman, 'A Purple Barium Copper Silicate Pigment from Early China,' *Studies in Conservation*, 37(3), 1992, pp. 145–154.
John Gage, *Colour and Meaning: Art, Science and Symbolism*, Thames & Hudson, UK, 2000.
Simon Garfield, *Mauve: How One Man Invented a Color that Changed the World*, W. W. Norton & Co., New York, 2002.
Laurence Sterne, *The Life and Opinions of Tristram Shandy, Gentleman*. Wordsworth Editions Ltd, UK, 1996.
William Harper Twelvetrees, ed., Tasmanian Department of Mines, *Stichtite: A New Tasmanian Mineral*. John Vail Government Printer, Hobart, 1914. http://www.mrt.tas.gov.au/mrtdoc/dominfo/download/GSREC02_OLD/GSREC02.pdf

The Things I Cannot Say

Louisa May Alcott, *Little Women*, Abbey Classics, Murrays Children's Books, UK, 1978.
Louisa May Alcott, *Good Wives*, Priory Books, Bridlington.
Simone de Beauvoir, *The Second Sex*, trans. Constance Borde and Sheila Malovany-Chevallier, Vintage, London, 2009.
Rebecca Goldstein, *Betraying Spinoza: The Renegade Jew Who Gave Us Modernity*, Schocken Books, New York, 2009.
Katherine Mansfield, *The Collected Letters of Katherine Mansfield 1903–1917*, Clarendon Press, Oxford, 1984.

Maiden Aunts

1. Virginia Nicholson, *Singled Out: How Two Million Women Survived Without Men After the First World War*, Penguin, London, 2008, pp. 28–29.

Blue Meat and Purple Language

1. 'Blue Meat and Purple Language', *The Northern Miner*, 23 October, 1919, p. 2. http://ttrove.nla.gov.au/ndp/del/article/82750089
2. 'At the Dance, Deep Purple Language. Trouble at Castlereagh', *The Nepean Times*, 10 November, 1928, p. 1. http://trove.nla.gov.au/ndp/del/article/100922157
3. 'Said Language Became Purple When He Quarreled with Wife', *Recorder*, 21 January, 1938, p. 1. http://trove.nla.gov.au/ndp/del/article/95939839
4. R. Stephens, J. Atkins and A. Kingston, 'Swearing as a Response to Pain', *Neuroreport,* August 5, 20(12), 2009, pp. 1056–60. http://ncbi.nlm.nih.gov/pubmed/19590391
5. William Shakespeare, *The Merry Wives of Windsor,* Act IV, Scene 1.
6. William Shakespeare, *Henry V,* Act IV, Scene 4.
7. William Shakespeare, *Othello,* Act I, Scene 1.
8. Virginia Woolf, *Mrs Dalloway,* Oxford Univerity Press, Oxford, 2008, p. 63.

Into the Whipstick

1. Lisa Baraitser, *Maternal Encounters: The Ethics of Interruption.* Routledge, London, 2009. See Chapter 4, 'Maternal Interruptions'. Also see an interesting discussion of Baraitser by Petra Bueskens and Julie Rodgers, and a new essay by Lisa Baraitser in Petra Bueskens, *Mothering and Psychoanalysis: Clinical, Sociological and Feminist Perspectives*, Demeter Press, Canada, 2009.
2. Susie Orbach and Luise Echenbaum, *What Do Women Want?*, HarperCollins, London, 1994.

Velvet

1. St Paul's Cathedral website. http://www.stpauls.co.uk/history-collections/history/jubilee/1935-george-v-silver

2   Drusilla Modjeska, 'Memoir Australia', in *Timepieces*, Picador, Sydney, 2002, p. 196.
3   Richard Holmes, 'A Meander through Memory and Forgetting', in *Memory: An Anthology*, eds Harriet Harvey Wood and A. S. Byatt, Vintage, UK, 2009, p. 95.
4   Lloyd Jones, *A History of Silence*, Text, Melbourne, Vic., 2013, p. 40.
5   Adam Phillips, 'The Forgetting Museum', in *Index on Censorship*, 34(2), 2005, pp. 34–37.
6   Endel Tulving, 'Episodic Memory: from Mind to Brain', in *Annual Review of Psychology*, 53, 2002, pp. 1–25.
7   Adam Phillips, 'The Forgetting Museum'.

Do You See What I See?

1   John Gage, *Colour in Art*, Thames & Hudson, London, 2006, p. 204.
2   ibid., p. 205.
3   Tracy Farr, 'The Sound of One Man Dying', in *Another 100 NZ Short Short Stories*, ed. Graeme Lay, Tandem Press, Auckland, 1998, p. 139.
4   Tracy Farr, 'The Blind Astronomer', in *The Best New Zealand Fiction Volume 1*, ed. Fiona Kidman, Vintage, Auckland, 2004, p. 27. First published in *Sport 28*, March 2002, pp. 135–142 http://nzetc.victoria.ac.nz//tm/scholarly/tei-Ba28Spo-t1-body-d18.html
5   ibid., p. 28.
6   Simon Ings, *The Eye: A Natural History*, Bloomsbury, London, 2007, p. 228.
7   ibid., p. 219.
8   John Gage, *Colour and Meaning: Art, Science and Symbolism*, Thames & Hudson, London, 2000, p. 136.
9   John Gage, *Colour and Culture: Practice and Meaning from Antiquity to Abstraction*, Thames & Hudson, London, 1995, p. 167.
10 Ings, *The Eye*, p. 213.
11 Philip Hensher, 'A. S. Byatt, The Art of Fiction No. 168', *The Paris Review*, No. 159, 2001. http://www.theparisreview.org/interviews/481/the-art-of-fiction-no-168-a-s-byatt
12 Gage, *Colour and Meaning*, p. 72.
13 Gage, *Colour in Art*, p. 147.
14 Gage, *Colour and Culture*, p. 80.
15 Gage, *Colour and Meaning*, p. 69.

16 ibid.
17 ibid.
18 Gage, *Colour and Culture*, p. 140.
19 ibid.
20 Gage, *Colour and Meaning*, p. 140.
21 Farr, 'The Blind Astronomer', p. 27.
22 ibid., p. 30.
23 ibid., pp. 27–30.
24 Patrick Trevor-Roper, *The World Through Blunted Sight: Inquiry into the Influence of Defective Vision on Art and Character*, revised edition, Souvenir Press, London, 1997.
25 Gage, *Colour and Culture*, p. 192.
26 Ings, *The Eye*, p. 193.
27 Margaret Visser, *The Way We Are*, Penguin, London, 1994, p. 237.
28 Gage, *Colour and Meaning*, p. 263.
29 ibid., p. 266.
30 Farr, 'The Sound of One Man Dying', p. 139.
31 Margaret Visser, *The Way We Are*, p. 239.
32 Mark Seymour, 'Do You See What I See', lyrics, *Human Frailty*, Mushroom Music, 1987.
33 Paul Kelly, 'I'd Rather Go Blind', *Words and Music*, Mushroom Music, 1998. In fact, in 'C90', the companion piece to 'I'd Rather Go Blind' in *How to Make Gravy* (Penguin, Melbourne, 2010, p. 238), Kelly indicates that he is referencing 'Etta James's aching "I'd Rather Go Blind"'.
34 Farr, 'The Blind Astronomer', p. 30.
35 Ings, *The Eye*, p. 13.
36 Farr, 'The Blind Astronomer', p. 26.
37 ibid.
38 ibid., p. 30.
39 Eva Isaksson, 'E-Accessible Astronomy Resources', *ASP Conference Series*, No. 432, 2010. http://arxiv.org/abs/1006.1803v1
40 Farr, 'The Blind Astronomer', p. 32.

Mary

1 Virginia Woolf, *The Diary of Virginia Woolf, Volume 4: 1931–35*, ed. Anne Olivier Bell, Hogarth Press, London, 1977, p. 24.
2 Iain Sinclair, *Edge of the Orison: In the Traces of John Clare's 'Journey Out of Essex'*, Penguin Books, London, 2006, p. 23.

3   Indebted to Nicolas Abraham's and Mária Török's notion of the crypt as developed in their book *The Wolf Man's Magic Word: A Cryptonymy*, trans. Nicholas Rand, University of Minnesota Press, Minneapolis, 2005.
4   Dorothy Hewett, *Greenhouse*, Big Smoke Books, Sydney, 1979, p. 40.
5   Dorothy Hewett, 'The Golden Mean' in *Dorothy Hewett: Collected Poems*, ed. William Grono, Fremantle Arts Centre Press, Fremantle, WA, 1995, p. 408.

The Trouble with Purple

1   Lewis Carroll, Chapter 5, 'Wool and Water', *Through the Looking Glass*. Macmillan, ebook, 2014, np.
2   National Geographic Society, *The Genographic Project*, 2015. http://genographic.nationalgeographic.com/about/
3   Cassandra Franklin-Barbajosa, 'In the Wake of the Phoenicians: DNA study reveals a Phoenician-Maltese link', *National Geographic Magazine* (online extra), October 2004. http://ngm.nationalgeographic.com/ngm/0410/feature2/online_extra.html
4   Marcus Vitruvius, *The Ten Books on Architecture*, Book VII, Ch. XIII, par. 1, trans. Morris Hickey Morgan, Dover Publications, New York, 1960, pp. 119–120.

The Red and the Blue

1   Adam McNicol, 'Anytime, Anywhere Dockers Claim Famous Finals Win at Geelong', AFL website. http://www.afl.com.au/news/2013-09-07/dockers-show-their-steel
2   AFL, 'Respect and Responsibility: What is the Respect and Responsibility Policy?', AFL Community, 2014. http://aflcommunityclub.com.au/index.php?id=750
3   AFL, 'Female Football', AFL Community, 2014. http://aflcommunityclub.com.au/index.php?id=495
4   Anna Krien, *Night Games: Sex, Power and Sport*, Black Inc., Collingwood, Vic., 2013, ebook.
5   Fremantle Dockers, 'Sirens Membership', Fremantle Dockers website, 2014. http://membership.fremantlefc.com.au/packages-prices/purple-army

6   Krien, *Night Games*, Loc. 1896.
7   Matt Price, *Way to Go: Sadness, Euphoria and the Fremantle Dockers*, Fremantle Arts Centre Press, Fremantle, WA, 2003.
8   Krien, *Night Games*, Loc. 1918.
9   Rosie Duffy, 'Margaret's Century', *Fremantle Dockers News &Media*, October 31 2014. http://www.fremantlefc.com.au/news/2014-10-31/margarets-milestone
10 Les Everett, *Fremantle Dockers: An Illustrated History*, Slattery Media Group, Richmond, Vic., 2014, p. 21.
11 Gervase A. Haimes, *Organizational Culture and Identity: A Case Study from the Australian Football League*, PhD thesis, Victoria University, 2006, pp. 154–155.
12 Mark Evans quoted in Michael Warner, *Herald Sun*, 'AFL Set to Launch Gay Pride Game to Tackle Homophobia During NAB Challenge', 4 March, 2015. www.heraldsun.com.au/sport/afl/afl-set-to-launch-gay-pride-game-to-tackle-homophobia-during-nab-challenge/story-fni5f22o-1227248255109
13 Callum Twomey, 'Dockers, Swans to Host NAB Challenge Pride Match', 5 March, 2015, AFL website. http://www.afl.com.au/news/2015-03-05/afl-announces-pride-match

Purple Impressions

1   John Russell letter to Tom Roberts, Winter 1890–91, from Bernard Smith, *Documents on Art and Taste in Australia: The Colonial Period, 1770–1914*, Oxford University Press, Melbourne, 1975, p. 201, quoted in Elena Taylor, *Australian Impressionists in France*, National Gallery of Victoria, Melbourne, Vic., 2013, p. 64.
2   'Colorants: Pigments versus Dyes', Lecture 12, PowerPoint presentation, 2001. http://www2.fiu.edu/~gardinal/class_syllabi/IDS4290%20FALL2010/Lecture%2012%20colored%20stuff.pdf
3   Michael Lloyd and Michael Desmond, *European and American Paintings and Sculptures 1870–1970 in the Australian National Gallery*, ANG, Canberra, 1992, p. 72. http://nga.gov.au/international Catalogue/Detail.cfm?ViewID=1&MnuID=1&GalID=ALL&SubViewID=2&IRN=29073
4   Johannes Itten, *The Art of Color: The Subjective Experience and Objective Rationale of Color*, trans. Ernst van Haagen, John Wiley & Sons, Inc., New York, 1960, reprinted 1973, p. 72.

NOTES AND REFERENCES

5   Luigina De Grandis, *Theory and Use of Color*, trans. John Gilbert, Harry N. Abrams, Inc., New York, 1986, p. 22.
6   Andrew Brown, 'Newton and Goethe on Colour' in *Homo Discens Project*. http://www.homodiscens.com/home/ways/perspicax/colr_vision_sub/art_colour_theory
7   Itten, *The Art of Color*, p. 13.
8   Liane Collot d'Herbois, *Light, Darkness and Colour in Painting Therapy*, Floris Books, Edinburgh, 1993, reprinted 2000, p. 239.
9   Johann Wolfgang von Goethe, *Theory of Colours*, trans. Charles Lock Eastlake, MIT Press, Cambridge, 1810, reprinted 1982, p. 141. http://en.wikipedia.org/wiki/Theory_of_Colours#Influence_on_the_arts
10 Patricia Sloane, ed., *Primary Sources: Selected Writings on Color from Aristotle to Albers*, Design Press, New York, 1991, p. xvi.
11 ibid., p. 123.
12 John Gage, *Colour and Meaning: Art, Science and Symbolism*, Thames & Hudson, London, 2000, p. 227.
13 James C. Marvis, ed., 'The Water-lily Pond – Symphony in Green', *Arch Gen Psychiatry*, 64(12), 2007, p. 1347. archpsyc.jamanetwork.com/article.aspx?articleid=482495
14 *Hemerocallis* is Greek for 'beauties of a day', a variety favoured by Monet for the fleeting lifespan of their blooms: Laurence Bertrand Dorléac, *Claude Monet*, ed. Alice Ertaud, Réunion des Musées Nationaux: Musée d'Orsay, Paris, 2010, p. 66.

Bruised

Alice Morgan, *What is Narrative Therapy? An Easy-to-read Introduction*, Dulwich Centre Publications, Adelaide, South Australia, 2000.

Jacqueline Wright, *Red Dirt Talking*, Fremantle Press, Fremantle, WA, 2013.

My Descent into Purple

1   The Christian Democratic Party (CDU) – a party with a conservative Catholic tradition – chose a Turkish-Muslim woman as their candidate in the 2013 federal elections – she won. There are eleven Turkish-born MPs and two African-born MPs in the German Parliament.

2   In 1933, the Nazi government used a similar law banning artists, communists, socialists and Jews from certain professions; they were later sent to concentration camps.
3   In the 1950s, the House Un-American Activities Committee blacklisted card-carrying communists or any sympathisers from working as actors, directors, screenwriters, etc.
4   Hanifa Deen, ed., *Sultana's Dream* (online magazine), May 2011 – April 2014. http://www.sultanasdream.com.au

Towards Metamorphosis

1   Jenny Joseph, 'Warning', first published 1961 in the BBC's magazine *The Listener*; in print in her *Selected Poems* (Bloodaxe, UK, 1993) and *Warning: When I Am an Old Woman I Shall Wear Purple* (Souvenir Press, UK, 1997); her reading of the poem is at http://www.youtube.com/watch?v=8cACbzanitg
2   Liz Byrski, *Getting On: Some Thoughts on Women and Ageing*, Momentum, ebook, 2012.
3   Valerie Monroe, 'What it Feels Like to Stop Getting Noticed', in *O, The Oprah Magazine*, March 2009. http://www.oprah.com/spirit/How-to-Deal-with-Aging-Valerie-Monroe-on-Getting-Older
4   M. E. Radina, A. Lynch, M. C. Stalp and L. K. Manning, '"When I Am an Old Woman, I Shall Wear Purple": Red Hatters Cope with Getting Old', in *Journal of Women & Aging*, 20(1–2), 2008, p. 100.
5   Hilary Mantel, 'Women Over 50 – The Invisible Generation', in *The Guardian*, 4 August 2009.
6   Red/Pink Hatters in WA information site, http://www.red-hatters-wa.net; *Red Hat Society* (US), redhatsociety.com
7   Stef Hayward, interviewed on ABC *Stateline* (n.d.), Red/Pink Hatters in WA information site.
8   'Margaret', in M. C. Stalp, M. E. Radina and A. Lynch, '"We Do it Cuz it's Fun": Gendered Fun and Leisure for Midlife Women through Red Hat Society Membership', in *Sociological Perspectives*, 51(2), 2008, p. 340.
9   Unnamed interviewee, in C. M. Yarnal, 'The Red Hat Society: Exploring the Role of Play, Liminality, and Communitas in Older Women's Lives', *Journal of Women & Aging*, 18(3), 2006, p. 64; Hayward, ABC *Stateline*.

10 Clema, in S. van Bohemen, L. van Zoonen and S. Aupers, 'Performing the "Fun" Self: How Members of the Red Hat Society Negotiate Cultural Discourses of Femininity and Ageing', in *European Journal of Cultural Studies*, 16(424), 2013, p. 430.
11 'Nora', in Stalp et al., p. 336.
12 Yarnal, 'The Red Hat Society', p. 64; *Red Hat Society* (US).
13 Stalp et al., p. 344.
14 Rebecca Wright, 'Local Red Hatters Ditch the Purple and Red, Start New Social Club', in *The Windsor Star*, 21 September 2013. http://blogs.windsorstar.com/life/local-red-hatters-ditch-the-purple-and-red-start-new-social-club
15 'Crabby Old Lady' (Ronni Bennett), 'How the Red Hatters Disappoint', in *Time Goes By*, blog, 1 February 2006. http://www.timegoesby.net/weblog/2006/02/how_the_red_hat.html
16 Comments by kenju and Jennifer Warwick, ibid.
17 Julia Twigg, 'Clothing, Age and the Body: A Critical Review', in *Ageing & Society*, 27, Cambridge University Press, UK, 2007, pp. 293–4. http://www.researchgate.net/publication/228344436_Clothing_age_and_the_body_a_critical_review
18 Ann Hunt, 'Review: Deca Dance, Batsheva Dance Company', stuff.co.nz, 22 February, 2014. http:// www.stuff.co.nz/dominion-post/culture/nz-festival-2014/9751895/Review-Deca-Dance-Batsheva-Dance-Company
19 William Yeoman, 'Hope is the Vital Key', *The West Australian*, 17 June, 2014.

Contributors

Liz Byrski is a novelist, non-fiction writer, former journalist and ABC broadcaster, with more than fifty years experience in the British and Australian media. She is the author of eight bestselling novels including *Gang of Four* and *Family Secrets*, and several non-fiction books including *In Love and War: Nursing Heroes* and *Remember Me*. Her books have been published in the UK, France and Germany. Liz has a PhD on the subject of women's fiction and lectures in professional and creative writing at Curtin University.

Lily Chan was born in Kyoto, raised in Narrogin, studied law at Murdoch University and now resides in Melbourne. *Toyo*, a memoir of her grandmother, was the recipient of the 2010 Peter Blazey Fellowship for a manuscript-in-progress, won the Dobbie Literary Award and was shortlisted for the Colin Roderick Award in 2013. Lily is at work on a second book and keeps an illustrated dream diary.

Amanda Curtin is the author of novels *Elemental* (shortlisted for the 2014 WA Premier's Book Awards) and *The Sinkings*, and a short story collection, *Inherited*, and has had short fiction published in *Griffith Review*, *Westerly*, *Southerly*, *Island* and *Indigo*. She is the current fiction editor for *Westerly* and is associated with Edith Cowan University as an adjunct lecturer. She will not entertain requests for performances on stage that do not involve her holding a book. Visit Amanda at www.amandacurtin.com

CONTRIBUTORS

Hanifa Deen is a Melbourne-based author who writes narrative non-fiction. Her titles include the award-winning *Caravanserai: Journey Among Australian Muslims*, *Broken Bangles* (shortlisted for the WA Premier's Book Award), *The Crescent and the Pen*, *The Jihad Seminar* (shortlisted for the Australian Human Rights Commission Non-Fiction Literary Award), *Ali Abdul v. The King* and *On the Trail of Taslima*. Hanifa is the founding editor of online magazine *Sultana's Dream*, www.sultanasdream.com.au. Visit Hanifa at www.hanifadeen.com.

Lucy Dougan is a widely published poet. Her books include *White Clay* and *Meanderthals* and *The Guardians*; and her prizes include the Mary Gilmore Award and the Alec Bolton Award. A past poetry editor of *HEAT* magazine, she now works for the Westerly Centre at UWA and is poetry edtior for the journal *Axon: Creative Explorations*. Her PhD, concerning representations of Naples, was awarded in 2010.

Sarah Drummond is the author of *Salt Story: of Sea Dogs and Fisherwomen*, a memoir and social history of south coast commercial estuarine fishers. Her shorter works are published in *Best Australian Essays*, *Overland*, *Indigo* journals and many other publications. Sarah lives on the south coast of Western Australia.

Tracy Farr is a novelist, short story writer, and former research scientist. In 2014, her debut novel *The Life and Loves of Lena Gaunt* was longlisted for the Miles Franklin Literary Award, and shortlisted for the WA Premier's Book Awards and the Barbara Jefferis Award. It will be published in the UK in 2016. Tracy was born in Melbourne but grew up in Perth, and studied science and arts at the University of WA. She lives in Wellington, New Zealand.

Deborah Hunn is a lecturer in the Department of Communication and Cultural Studies at Curtin University. Her publications include short stories, critical essays and reviews. She blogs at deborahhunn.wordpress.com/

Toni Jordan's debut novel, the international bestseller *Addition*, was published in 2008, chosen for the Richard and Judy Bookclub and longlisted for the Miles Franklin award. Her second novel, *Fall Girl*, was published in Australia, the UK, France, Germany and Taiwan, and has been optioned for film. Her latest novel, *Nine Days*, was awarded Best Fiction at the 2012 Indie Awards, was shortlisted for the ABIA Best General Fiction award and was named by Kirkus Review in the top ten Historical Novels of 2013. Toni has been widely published in newspapers and magazines.

Natasha Lester is the award-winning author of *What is Left Over, After* and *If I Should Lose You*. Her third book will be published in early 2016. She has been described by *The Age* newspaper as 'a remarkable Australian talent'. When she's not writing, Natasha teaches creative writing and plays dress-ups with her three children.

Anne Manne is a Melbourne writer. She was a regular columnist for *The Australian* and *The Age*, and writes essays on contemporary life for *The Monthly* and other publications. Her book *Motherhood: How Should We Care for Our Children?* was a finalist in the Walkley Award for Best Non-Fiction Book. She has also written a *Quarterly Essay: Love and Money; The Family and The Free Market*, and a memoir, *So This is Life: Scenes from a Country Childhood*. Her most recent book is *The Life of I: The New Culture of Narcissism*.

Rachel Robertson is a lecturer in the School of Media, Culture and Creative Arts at Curtin University. Her memoir *Reaching One Thousand* was shortlisted for the National Biography Award in 2013 and she won the *Australian Book Review* Calibre Award for Outstanding Essay in 2008. Her personal essays have been published in journals and anthologies such as *Life Writing, Westerly, Griffith Review* and *Best Australian Essays*. Her research interests include critical disability studies, Australian literature, motherhood studies, life writing and ethics.

Rosemary Stevens has worked in London for a publisher and literary agent and in Asia as a travel writer. She currently teaches creative and professional writing at Curtin University and was assistant editor for *Griffith Review*'s 2015 summer issue *Looking West 47*, focusing on Western Australia. Her short stories, travel books and articles have been published throughout Australasia.

Annamaria Weldon, author of *The Lake's Apprentice*, won the inaugural Nature Conservancy Australia's Prize for Nature Writing (2011). Her poems, non-fiction, reviews and short stories have been published in Australian literary journals, broadcast on the ABC's Radio National and featured in collaborations across art disciplines. Earlier poetry collections are *The Roof Milkers* and *Ropes of Sand*.

Jacqueline Wright has been published in *Bodylines, Summer Readings, Griffith Review, Kimberley Stories, Summer Lovin', Knitting and Other Stories* and *Griffith Review*'s *Looking West*. Her first novel, *Red Dirt Talking*, written as part of a creative arts doctorate at Curtin University, earned her first prize in the T. A. G. Hungerford Award (2010), was longlisted for the Miles Franklin Literary Award (2013) and shortlisted for the Dobbie Literary Award (2013). Parts of *Red Dirt Talking* have been adapted for radio and stage. Jacqueline works as a producer for *Mornings* at ABC Kimberley.

Acknowledgments

The editors would like to thank the writers whose contributions make up this diverse anthology; without their imagination and generosity the idea would not have grown wings. Many thanks, too, to research assistant Eva Bujalka for early research on the colour purple. We are grateful to the School of Media, Culture and Creative Arts at Curtin University for support for this project. And last, but by no means least, to our editor and publisher Georgia Richter and the entire team at Fremantle Press with whom it has been such a pleasure to work.

ACKNOWLEDGEMENTS

The publisher gratefully acknowledges permission to reproduce quotations from the following works: Liz Byrski © 2013, *Getting On: Some Thoughts on Women and Ageing*. Reprinted by kind permission of Momentum; Tracy Farr, 'The Sound of One Man Dying' first appeared in *Another 100 NZ Short Short Stories*, ed. Graeme Lay, Tandem Press, Auckland, 1998); Rebecca Goldstein © 2009, *Betraying Spinoza: The Renegade Jew Who Gave Us Modernity*. Reprinted by kind permission of Schocken Books; John Gage © 2006, *Colour in Art*, reprinted by kind permission of Thames & Hudson Ltd, London; John Gage © 1999, *Colour and Meaning*, reprinted by kind permission of Thames & Hudson Ltd, London; John Gage © 1993, *Colour and Culture*, reprinted by kind permission of Thames & Hudson Ltd, London; Richard Holmes © 2009, 'A Meander through Memory and Forgetting' in *Memory: An Anthology*, Harriet Harvey Wood and A. S. Byatt, eds, published by Chatto & Windus and reproduced by permission of The Random House Group Ltd; Simon Ings © 2008, *The Eye: A Natural History*, Bloomsbury Publishing Plc.; Lloyd Jones © 2013, *A History of Silence*, published by Text and reproduced with permission from the Text Publishing Company Pty Ltd; Adam Phillips © 2005, 'The Forgetting Museum', first published in *Index on Censorship 2*, and reproduced by permission of the author.

More great reads

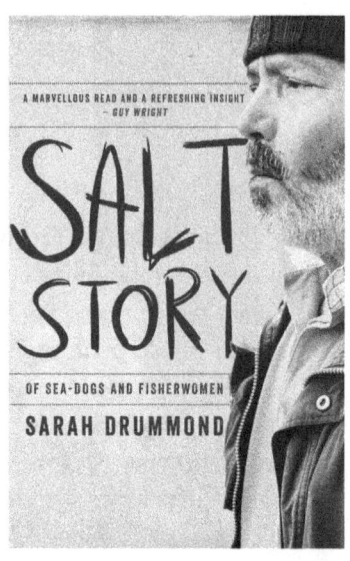

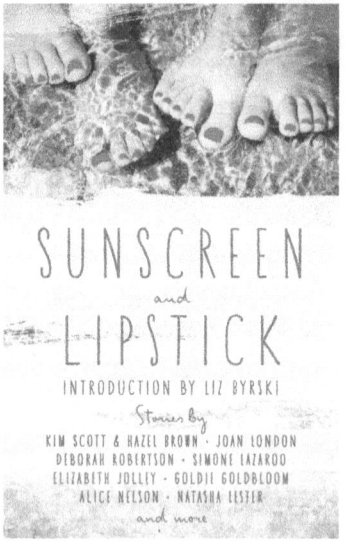

Available from fremantlepress.com.au

from Fremantle Press

and all good bookstores

First published 2015 by
FREMANTLE PRESS
25 Quarry Street, Fremantle 6160
(PO Box 158, North Fremantle 6159)
Western Australia
www.fremantlepress.com.au

Also available as an ebook.

Copyright © individual contributors, 2015.

The moral rights of the authors have been asserted.

This book is copyright. Apart from any fair dealing for the purpose of private study, research, criticism or review, as permitted under the Copyright Act, no part may be reproduced by any process without written permission. Enquiries should be made to the publisher.

Editors Liz Byrski and Rachel Robertson
Consultant editor Georgia Richter
Cover image Wilkie Productions

A catalogue record for this book is available from the National Library of Australia

ISBN: 9781925163094 (paperback)
ISBN: 9781925163117 (ebook)

Fremantle Press is supported by the Western Australian State Government through the Department of Cultural Industries, Tourism and Sport.

Publication of this title was assisted by the Commonwealth Government through Creative Australia, its arts funding and advisory body.

www.ingramcontent.com/pod-product-compliance
Lightning Source LLC
Chambersburg PA
CBHW021155160426
43194CB00007B/752